# Contents

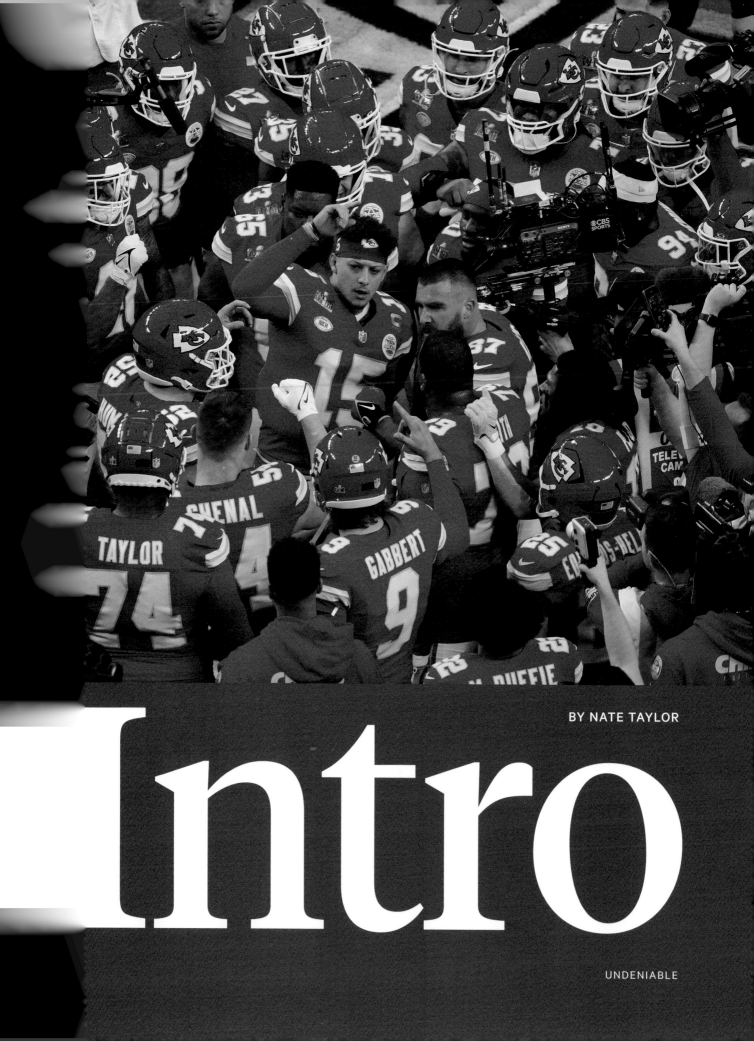

BY NATE TAYLOR

# Intro

UNDENIABLE

Red, yellow and white confetti falling at Allegiant Stadium in Las Vegas was the confirmation of their coronation. Once again, the Kansas City Chiefs experienced the feeling only one team achieves in an NFL season, accomplishing a daunting objective that leads to an exhilarating sensation.

With their 25-22 overtime victory over the San Francisco 49ers in Super Bowl LVIII, the Chiefs became the NFL's first repeat champion in two decades. The win cemented a golden era for the franchise and its status as one of the true dynasties in the league's 104-year history.

"It's the start of one," Patrick Mahomes insisted. "We're not done."

To secure their third Lombardi Trophy in five years, the Chiefs had to overcome the worst regular season in the Andy Reid-Patrick Mahomes era as well as the most treacherous postseason path.

The Chiefs, the AFC's No. 3 seed, dominated the Miami Dolphins in freezing conditions, a game in which Reid coached with icicles hanging off his mustache. Then, in the first road playoff game of Mahomes' seven-year career, the Chiefs rallied in the second half for a 27-24 victory, their defense holding the Buffalo Bills scoreless in the fourth quarter. They reached the Super Bowl with another road victory, a 17-10 win over league MVP Lamar Jackson and the Baltimore Ravens, who entered the postseason with the NFL's best record.

Mahomes led the winning 75-yard drive in overtime against the 49ers, capping it with a 3-yard touchdown pass to Mecole Hardman. The Chiefs rallied from a 10-0 deficit and got the score they needed on the final drive of the game.

Mahomes won his third Super Bowl MVP award, but make no mistake, defense was the backbone of the 2023 Chiefs.

"This is the best defense I've ever played with," tight end Travis Kelce said midway through the season. "Honestly, they've been saving us in a lot of situations."

No opponent scored 30 points on coordinator Steve Spagnuolo's unit, which allowed the fewest second-half points in the league. Defensive tackle Chris Jones and defensive end George Karlaftis led the team with 10 1/2 sacks. Spagnuolo's defense benefited from career-best seasons from several players, including cornerbacks L'Jarius Sneed and Trent McDuffie, safety Justin Reid and defensive end Charles Omenihu.

"Seeing this defense all year long, I've learned that sometimes I've got to let them play, let them be the show," Mahomes said.

Mahomes, the league's most talented quarterback, demonstrated his leadership, creativity and acumen all season but played his best when the Chiefs needed it in January and February.

"It's hard to describe someone that good," general manager Brett Veach said. "He's a legend. He's a blessing."

Kelce, an 11-year veteran, also had his best moments in the postseason as he overcame lingering injuries to his knee and ankle to pass Hall of Fame receiver Jerry Rice for the most postseason receptions in NFL history.

"We got the best quarterback in the world," Chiefs linebacker Drue Tranquill said. "We got the best tight end in the world. We got the best coach in the world. We got the best defensive coordinator in the world. We got the best general manager in the world.

"When you have all of that? It's only a matter of time."

But it took time for the defending champions to put it all together this time. The Chiefs stumbled to start the season, losing to the Detroit Lions in the league's opening night game. All-Pros Kelce and Jones didn't play — Kelce because of a knee injury and Jones because he was holding out. But the Chiefs lost because of eight dropped passes, the two most egregious by wide receiver Kadarius Toney. Dropped passes would be a recurring problem through the regular season as Kansas City led the NFL with 44.

Mahomes and company won their next six games and went into their bye week with a 7-2 record after shutting down the high-powered Dolphins offense in Frankfurt, Germany. But they lost four of their next six as the errors piled up. The low point came on Christmas Day at Arrowhead Stadium with an ugly 20-14 loss to the Las Vegas Raiders.

Veach is convinced that without that Christmas Day humbling, there's no way the Chiefs would have made it to the Super Bowl.

"Something was off," Veach said. "That loss, I think it really hit us. It allowed the whole organization to take a look in the mirror."

That self-evaluation on the cusp of the playoffs resulted in Reid condensing the playbook and simplifying the game plan.

Running back Isiah Pacheco ran the ball with determination, rookie Rashee Rice blossomed into a No. 1 wide receiver and the offensive line jelled at the right time. The mistakes that hamstrung the offense during the regular season disappeared. And the Chiefs didn't lose again.

"We might not be the prettiest, but we're going to battle," Reid said. "That's the personality of this team."

A team that once hung its hat on high-powered offense and Mahomes' improvisational passing, needed to change its personality this season. From day one of training camp on July 18 until the end of overtime in the Super Bowl on Feb. 11, the Chiefs maintained their status as the league's best by earning a second consecutive championship not with flash but through gritty perseverance. ∎

---

**LEFT:** Patrick Mahomes leads a team huddle prior to Super Bowl XVIII in Las Vegas.

# Super Bowl

# LVIII

# 'We're Not Done'

Patrick Mahomes and Chiefs Do It Again in Thrilling OT Win

BY NATE TAYLOR

Several men wearing red Kansas City Chiefs jerseys began crying.

When the seventh-longest game in NFL history concluded, center Creed Humphrey ripped his helmet off, his tears beginning to fall. Malik Herring, a three-year defensive end, fell to his knees at midfield at Allegiant Stadium, his emotions overwhelming him. Even before the Chiefs' final drive of the season, Nick Allegretti, the backup left guard who started in place of All-Pro Joe Thuney, had tears in his eyes. Rookie Rashee Rice wept when he bear-hugged his coach, Andy Reid.

The man who didn't cry Sunday night, who simply exhaled — over and over and over again — was the NFL's most talented quarterback, the league's biggest game-altering superstar, the MVP of Super Bowl LVIII: Patrick Mahomes.

Mahomes was the first person to hug receiver Mecole Hardman, the teammate who caught the game-winning touchdown pass. Then Mahomes ran to the Chiefs' sideline, tossed his helmet and fell to the turf, rolling over on his back, his hands on his head, just above his red headband.

Mahomes' final pass, an easy 3-yard, walk-off touchdown to Hardman, who was wide open in the corner of the end zone, finished the longest season in the Chiefs' 64-year history with an unforgettable 25-22 comeback victory over the San Francisco 49ers in overtime in front of 61,629 fans in the NFL's first Super Bowl in Las Vegas. The Chiefs claimed their third Lombardi Trophy in five years.

Once Mahomes stood up and collected his thoughts, he delivered yet another declarative message for the rest of the league when asked if the Chiefs are a dynasty.

"It's the start of one," Mahomes said before he and his teammates hoisted their newest Lombardi Trophy. "We're not done."

In overtime, the Chiefs defense employed one of its best blitzes to force the 49ers to kick a field goal. Then, during a do-or-die drive, Mahomes orchestrated a 13-play sequence that produced his most memorable game-winning drive. The Chiefs celebrated becoming the NFL's first repeat champion in two decades by sprinting from their bench and into one another's arms, similar to school children hearing the final bell of the spring semester.

"This is one of the greatest teams of all time," said tight end Travis Kelce, an 11-year veteran and the team's longest-tenured player. "To go back-to-back is another tier. At this point in my career, I just enjoy coming into (the Chiefs' facility) because I know I'm closer to not playing than I am to keep playing. I just cherish every single moment."

Repeating as Super Bowl champion is one of the hardest things to do in the NFL. The Chiefs became just the ninth team to do it. They did so after posting the worst regular season in the Andy Reid—Mahomes era. And they needed to navigate their toughest playoff path as well.

As the AFC's No. 3 seed, the Chiefs dominated the Miami Dolphins in freezing conditions. Then, in the first road playoff game of Mahomes' seven-year career, the Chiefs rallied in the second half for a 27-24 victory, their defense holding the Buffalo Bills scoreless in the fourth quarter. They reached the Super Bowl with another road victory, a 17-10 win over league MVP Lamar Jackson and the Baltimore Ravens, who entered the postseason with the NFL's best record.

Aaron Schatz, the chief analytics officer of FTN Network and inventor of DVOA, said the Chiefs faced the hardest postseason road to a championship ever, based on the regular-season DVOA of their opponents.

"The journey we had to take, I think, (makes this) more satisfying than the previous Super Bowls," pass rusher Chris Jones said.

This season, a team that was once known for its high-powered offense and Mahomes' improvisational passing needed to change its personality. Mahomes said Sunday's game was symbolic of the Chiefs' season.

The 49ers built a 10-point lead, scoring their first touchdown on a trick play. Quarterback Brock Purdy threw a short pass behind the line of scrimmage to receiver Jauan Jennings, who completed an across-the-field pass to running back Christian McCaffrey, who sprinted untouched into the end zone for a 21-yard score.

RIGHT: Patrick Mahomes hoists the Lombardi Trophy following Super Bowl XVIII. The Chiefs quarterback was named the MVP after leading Kansas City to its third championship in five seasons.

> *"I hope people remember not only the greatness that we had on the field but the way that we battled. It's not always pretty."*

The Chiefs showed their frustration on the sideline. Kelce shoved and screamed at Reid for taking him out of the game. Running back Isiah Pacheco shook his head after he fumbled inside the 49ers' 10-yard line. Mahomes often felt pressure in the first half because the 49ers' four-man pass rush — defensive ends Nick Bosa and Chase Young and defensive tackles Arik Armstead and Javon Hargrave — dominated the Chiefs' offensive line. When halftime began, the Chiefs trotted into the locker room having scored just three points.

"I hope people remember not only the greatness that we had on the field but the way that we battled," Mahomes said. "It's not always pretty."

The most consistent unit for the Chiefs on Sunday once again was the defense, led by coordinator Steve Spagnuolo.

No opponent this season scored 30 points on Spagnuolo's unit, which allowed the fewest second-half points in the league. The Chiefs held the 49ers to 12 points in the final three quarters. Linebacker Leo Chenal even blocked the extra-point attempt after the 49ers' lone touchdown after halftime. Although Jones never sacked Purdy, he pressured him throughout the second half, hitting the quarterback twice. Spagnuolo increased his blitzes, too, to better collapse the pocket. Six defenders hit Purdy. The Chiefs defense generated a season-high nine unblocked pressures, all of which came on blitzes, according to Next Gen Stats.

"That's what we do, baby. We go on pressure, from left, right, center," safety Justin Reid said. "I've said it since training camp: This is the most intelligent defense that I've been a part of, but also physically dominant. Guys know the checks and calls and there's nobody who is scared to tackle. You want to run the ball to the edge, our corners are going to cut you in half. You want to run it down the middle, the safeties and linebackers are coming downhill.

**LEFT:** Patrick Mahomes hugs receiver Mecole Hardman after Hardman's 3-yard, game-winning touchdown reception.

*"Playing for the guy next to you, we grew up together, man. Guys have been in the same scheme for three or four years. We wanted it for the brother next to us more than anything else."*

"You match that with the ability of what Spags puts together in the game plan, it just puts us in a position to be successful."

The 49ers, led by coach Kyle Shanahan, made an interesting decision when they won the coin toss before the start of overtime. They decided to take the ball first, allowing the Chiefs offense to use all four downs if necessary to produce either a game-winning or game-tying score once they had the ball.

"I think, as a defensive player, it's a little disrespectful," linebacker Nick Bolton said. "Playing for the guy next to you, we grew up together, man. Guys have been in the same scheme for three or four years. We wanted it for the brother next to us more than anything else."

Spagnuolo broke his own play-calling tendency on the Chiefs' final defensive play, a third-and-5 snap from the 9-yard line. The Chiefs surprised Purdy with a Cover 0 blitz. The secondary — including cornerback Trent McDuffie and safeties Mike Edwards and Chamarri Conner — covered the 49ers' skill-position players well, allowing Jones to hit Purdy, who threw an incompletion.

"We had that as a third-down call throughout the game and we couldn't get it," Spagnuolo said. "We had it called one time and I think they went offside, so you just tuck it in your back pocket. I figured, 'Hey, it's a critical time, so pull it out.' The guys did a nice job."

After the game, Spagnuolo verbalized a thought many Chiefs fans must have had at the same time.

"Thank God we have Patrick Mahomes, that's for sure," Spagnuolo said.

With less than two minutes left in regulation, Mahomes led the Chiefs on a game-tying drive, going 64 yards before kicker Harrison Butker made the tying 29-yard field goal.

Just before the Chiefs' drive in overtime, offensive coordinator Matt Nagy and quarterbacks coach David

**LEFT:** Tight end Travis Kelce carries the ball against the 49ers. Kelce's nine catches for 93 yards led all Chiefs receivers.

## "Obviously, Coach Reid, man. He knows when to call those plays at the right time. I believe he's the best coach of all time."

Girardi reminded Mahomes of one of his underrated skills: *"Use your legs as a weapon at the right moments."*

Mahomes did. He led the Chiefs with 66 rushing yards on nine attempts. He fooled Bosa with a run-pass option play to gain 8 yards on a fourth-and-inches play. On another short-yardage play, a third-and-1 snap inside 49ers territory, Mahomes scrambled up the middle for a 19-yard gain.

"I don't know why guys don't spy him," Reid said of Mahomes.

Mahomes went 8-for-8 on the final drive, completing passes to five teammates — Pacheco, Kelce and receivers Marquez Valdes-Scantling, Rice and Hardman.

"It was an up-and-down year, but when our backs were against the wall, the guys got it done — Marquez, Mecole coming in midseason, Travis, Pat, Rashee, J-Wat (receiver Justin Watson), Pop (Pacheco) and the guys I'm honored to play with on the offensive line," Allegretti said. "It's such an awesome, awesome experience to be a part of this team."

The final play call included the phrase "Tom and Jerry," a misdirection play that Mahomes knew was going to work.

Using the same motion as "Corndog," which the Chiefs had used for a touchdown in last year's Super Bowl win, Hardman went in motion to the left, then pivoted hard in the opposite direction. Kelce, who was on the same side of the formation, was used as a decoy as he attracted the attention of the 49ers' last perimeter defender, cornerback Charvarius Ward.

"Obviously, Coach Reid, man," Mahomes said. "He knows when to call those plays at the right time. I believe he's the best coach of all time.

"I know he doesn't have the trophies yet — and I have a lot of respect for some of those great coaches — but the way he's able to navigate every single team he has, and continues to have success no matter where he's at, for me, he brings out the best in me because he

**RIGHT:** Patrick Mahomes celebrates after leading the Chiefs' game-winning touchdown drive in overtime.

*"I'm going to celebrate at the parade and I'm going to do whatever I can to be back in this game next year, trying to go for that three-peat."*

lets me be me. I don't think I'd be the quarterback I am if I didn't have Coach Reid."

The Chiefs, who lost five of eight to fall to 9-6 in late December, maintained their status as the league's best by earning a second consecutive championship with gritty resolve.

Mahomes showed his leadership, creativity and acumen all season. But he played his absolute best when the Chiefs needed it in January and February.

"I'm going to celebrate at the parade (in Kansas City on Wednesday) and I'm going to do whatever I can to be back in this game next year, trying to go for that three-peat," Mahomes said.

"I'm going to celebrate with my guys, because of how we've done this. But then we're going to work our way back to this game next year." ■

**RIGHT:** Patrick Mahomes moved Kansas City downfield with his legs as well as his arm in Super Bowl XVIII, leading the Chiefs with 66 rushing yards on nine attempts.

**LEFT:** In a crucial play, the Chiefs blocked 49ers kicker Jake Moody's extra point attempt early in the second quarter.

# Wildest Dreams

Mecole Hardman Caps Chiefs Return with Super Bowl-Clinching Touchdown, Not That He Remembers

BY ZAK KEEFER

After Mecole Hardman's three-yard touchdown grab clinched the Kansas City Chiefs' third Super Bowl win in five seasons, it all went dark.

"I blacked out," Hardman said on the Allegiant Stadium field an hour later. "After I caught it, I can't remember a thing that happened next."

What happened next: a mob of teammates rushed towards him while the elation of back-to-back world championships started to sink in. Same as the previous two, Kansas City's 25-22 overtime win over the San Francisco 49ers in Super Bowl LVIII required a 10-point second-half comeback, and again, Andy Reid, the Chiefs' veteran head coach, was at his best, pulling the right strings as offensive play-caller amid a 13-play 75-yard drive in overtime that culminated with Mahomes hitting Hardman for the walk-off score.

All of the Chiefs knew what had just happened, and what it meant.

Except Hardman. For a few moments, the fifth-year receiver was in a daze of disbelief. He held the football up with his right hand. Mahomes darted towards him. A sea of red followed.

"Can I tell a quick funny story?" the quarterback said later, interrupting Hardman's postgame interview on NFL Network. "I threw a touchdown to this dude at the end of the game, and he looked at me and he had no idea. I said, 'Dude, we just won the Super Bowl.' He didn't even celebrate at the beginning."

"I swear," Hardman said, "the first thing I remember is Pat yelling at me, saying, 'Bro, you a champion!'"

For Hardman, it was a surreal moment. Nothing about his past two years hinted this was coming; not after the Chiefs let him walk in free agency last spring, not after he signed with the New York Jets only to barely get on the field.

Certainly not after the biggest scare of all, a rare groin injury suffered in 2022 that Hardman later revealed kept him in the hospital for 10 days, unable to walk for five. An osteitis pubis diagnosis cost Hardman nine games last season. After returning, Hardman tore his groin during the 2022 AFC Championship Game, sidelining him from last year's Super Bowl win over the Eagles.

"Scary as hell," he called the ordeal.

It would pave the way for his exit from Kansas City in the spring, but that wouldn't last long. Never able to get on the same page with the Jets' coaches, he made all of one catch in five games. Hardman landed back in Kansas City in October after the teams agreed to swap late-round picks. The Chiefs needed receiver help. And Hardman, if nothing else, was a familiar face.

According to Reid, Hardman was succinct with the coaching staff when he returned to the Chiefs' practice facility: "Hey, I just wanna help you guys win." But it would take time.

"A roller coaster," Hardman called the last few years. "A lot of ups and downs. I was going through a lot, especially with the injury, trying to start over with a new team, and didn't really play. Kansas City welcomed me back with open arms."

Entering Sunday, Hardman had caught just 17 passes since returning, including only two in the Chiefs' playoff run. But in Super Bowl LVIII, he finished with three receptions for 57 yards and the game-winning score, the team's second-leading receiver behind tight end Travis Kelce.

Before the clincher, Hardman's biggest moment came early in the second quarter when he snuck behind the 49ers' secondary for a 52-yard catch — Kansas City's longest play all night. But an Isiah Pacheco fumble one play later on the 49ers' 9-yard-line left the Chiefs without any points.

The play that won Sunday's Super Bowl, which goes by the name "Tom and Jerry," is a cousin of the one Reid dialed up in the fourth quarter of last year's Super Bowl. That one, affectionately called "corn-dog," starts with a receiver going in quick motion, which helps Mahomes identify whether the defense is in man coverage or zone. Last year it resulted in a short throw to a wide-open Kadarius Toney that tied the game.

The Chiefs love "Tom and Jerry" against man coverage because it calls for a tight end to run a corner route, and if that tight end is Kelce, that usually means two defenders follow him. That's what happened Sunday night, if only for a split second. But it was enough to free up Hardman, who peeled into the flat untouched.

RIGHT: Patrick Mahomes embraces receiver Mecole Hardman after Hardman's game-winning touchdown catch.

> *"Man, you dream about that as a kid, making these game-winning catches, but I don't think I ever dreamed about doing it in the Super Bowl. The biggest game? I hope one of the equipment guys got that football, because I need to get that back."*

It was one of the easiest balls Mahomes threw all night.

"I knew," Hardman said. "I knew they were gonna double Trav, and as soon as I saw the corner drop off, I knew I was getting the ball."

According to fellow receiver Marquez Valdes-Scantling, if Mahomes had Hardman continued his motion, the play would have been a jet sweep to the other side of the field. "And if it's a jet sweep, he walks in the other way," Valdes-Scantling said in a raucous postgame locker room, cigar dangling from his mouth. "Either way, seals the game."

Teammates who saw Hardman's struggle up close were thrilled for him Sunday night.

"I've played with Mecole for a long time," Mahomes said. "He's always ready for the moment ... just like last year, you never know how it's gonna be."

"I knew we were gonna need him at some point," Valdes-Scantling said.

"Shoot, when you talking about a dude who's been injured, who's been trying to figure it out this year?" cornerback Trent McDuffie said. "Man, so proud of him. So proud of that guy."

While it all soaked in — another championship, the culmination of a trying two years — Hardman stood on the field, asking one last question: Who has the football?

"Man, you dream about that as a kid, making these game-winning catches, but I don't think I ever dreamed about doing it in the Super Bowl," he said. "The biggest game? I hope one of the equipment guys got that football, because I need to get that back." ∎

**LEFT:** Receiver Mecole Hardman, who returned to the Chiefs in October 2023 after signing with the New York Jets in the offseason, proved the unlikely hero for Kansas City.

# Road to the Title

# Andy Reid

**Why the Chiefs Coach Runs the NFL's Hardest Training Camp**

BY NATE TAYLOR ———————— AUGUST 18, 2023

In the NFL, gone are the days of grueling two-a-day practices, when players spent just as much time outside in the heat as they did in meetings and film sessions. This year, 25 teams opted to forgo a traditional training camp, choosing to stay home — at practice facilities, home stadiums or sites within 10 miles of headquarters.

The Kansas City Chiefs are an exception, one of just five teams that conducted camp on a college campus. Everyone in the Chiefs organization — players, coaches and executives — knows that as long as Andy Reid is their coach, the team will always start camp at Missouri Western State, or at least some college.

"I love being up here," Reid said last month. "I look forward to it."

Players agree that Reid, a future Hall of Famer at age 65, runs the league's most difficult camp. Since 2013, when he joined Kansas City after 13 years in Philadelphia, veteran Chiefs players have tried their best to warn rookies and other newcomers about Camp Reid's rigorous, old-school style.

"How hard could it be?" new left tackle Donovan Smith asked through a smile in June.

Nine weeks later, Smith was still smiling, but he acknowledged his teammates were right: "It's definitely an adjustment here. We definitely work our tails off."

Without fail every year, many of those new players, drenched in sweat and near extreme exhaustion, ask a version of the same question: *Why does Reid make camp this hard?* The answers come through experience.

———————

**Matt Nagy, offensive coordinator (seventh camp tour):** I've heard the war stories of that 1999 camp, Coach's first year in Philadelphia, from guys like (Eric Bieniemy), Doug Pederson and Brad Childress. I've heard there's never been a camp in the history of the NFL that's been as hard as that camp. I think Coach kind of liked that.

**Khalen Saunders, former defensive tackle (four tours):** The first thing that comes to mind is precision and no wasted reps.

**Nagy:** When (Bieniemy) talks about how hard something is, you know it's hard.

**Donovan Smith (first tour):** A lot of plays. We run a lot of plays.

**Saunders:** You're getting, like, 200 plays a day — and that's two games worth.

**Blaine Gabbert, quarterback (first tour):** It's an old-school method. It's refreshing. It's simple.

**Richie James, receiver (first tour):** As a receiver, it's brutal, for sure. You run a lot.

**Connor Embree, receivers coach (fifth tour):** There's no easy days. It's not like other places around the league, where you might be a 10-year vet and get a day off here and there. If you're healthy, you're going — and we're going hard and long.

**Drue Tranquill, linebacker (first tour):** It's a lot tougher than the previous four camps I've been a part of, for sure. He maximizes every minute of on-field time. The CBA says we get four hours (each day), we're going to be on the field for exactly four hours.

**Mitchell Schwartz, former right tackle (four tours):** He has the reps just generally set up a bit different. The first week or two of camp, most coaches have reps more evenly spaced out. He just starts right away — the ones are getting eight reps, the twos are getting four or five reps and the threes are getting two reps. That catches people's eyes.

**Justin Reid, safety (second tour):** I came in prepared this year. Last year, that first week or two, was just very fast. It's mentally challenging. The practices are way faster than any of the games ever are.

**Tranquill:** He grinds you. Sometimes you just feel like a turtle walking off the field.

**Nagy:** Last year, (former receiver) JuJu (Smith-Schuster) was laying on the turf in the indoor field and tweeted out, "That's the hardest practice I've ever had." I was like, "Dude, that's, like, nothing compared to what you're about to walk into."

**Dave Toub, special teams coordinator (13th tour):** He's not going to change his ways. You can't knock it, his success.

**Mike DeVito, former defensive end (three tours):** He's accounted for everything. In 2013, when I got there, I knew right away we were going to win. I could see how systematic he was. Everything had a purpose.

RIGHT: Patrick Mahomes throws while head coach Andy Reid observes during the Chiefs' 2023 training camp at Missouri Western State University.

**Mark Donovan, team president (16th tour):** The process brings him joy.

**Tranquill:** That picture of the Super Bowl ring is at the start of every single slide of every presentation.

**Donovan:** With the uniform stuff, you tuck your jersey, there's no initials, no triple names. You go to just about any other team, it's like, "If the guy wants something on his jersey, just give it to them to keep them happy." That's not how we do things.

**DeVito:** One of his rules is you cannot put your helmet on the ground. You have to keep your helmet in your hand. I was like, "That just seems so arbitrary." Then, you found out there was a time in Philly when one of his starting receivers ran a route, went out of bounds and tripped over a helmet and missed games because of it.

**Donovan:** The first year, before the players came in, he walked around the field. He goes, "Can you come down?" I come down. He goes, "Can you look at our goal post?" I look out. He goes, "Can you imagine a player coming in here and seeing the chipped paint on that goal post? How does that reflect on our team, our organization?" I'm like, "Got it, let's go paint the goal posts." He wants the players to know they're in a first-class organization.

**Travis Kelce, tight end (10th tour):** It's not an easy thing to get a bunch of grown men to stay disciplined. The welcome-to-the-league moment with Coach Reid was just that eyebrow he gives you, man. You're like, "All right, I better pick it up."

**Donovan:** Travis is the guy that's like, "That (route) won't fly with Andy. Do it this way."

**Marquez Valdes-Scantling, receiver (second tour):** Coach Reid doesn't have a lot of emotion. If you do get some emotion out of him, it's one of those, "Oooh, I might've messed up, for real." I have gotten that. It was in the meeting room. It's not a good feeling.

**Schwartz:** If he has to criticize you, even in a team setting where he's showing plays where he has to criticize someone, he's doing it to teach something to the group.

**Saunders:** It's mind-blowing how he says the exact same things, almost like a tape recorder. Then he's got his catchphrases, the "son-of-a-buck," "son-on-a-gun" and "doggone it." We can probably put a money line on which one he's going to say in the meeting.

**Donovan:** One of things that's really powerful about him is (his) father figure (status). You want to do right by your father. When your dad gives you a look, you go,

RIGHT: While most NFL teams now opt to forgo traditional training camps, Andy Reid embraces an old-school approach.

"OK." I've experienced it. For the players, they just want to do right by him.

---

*Some of the most demanding elements of Reid's camps are the "long drive" team periods, which occur once the novelty of camp has worn off and with the first preseason game still a few days away. The projected starters can be on the field for as many as 20 repetitions in less than 15 minutes.*

**Jeff Allen, former offensive lineman (four tours):** My favorite day in camp was always Day 1 of pads. After that, I just wanted to fast-forward to the season.

**Valdes-Scantling:** The long-drive drill sucks. It's going to suck every time we do it — and we do it quite a bit.

**Schwartz:** It's definitely weird. It's one of the only periods in practice that feels somewhat realistic.

**Saunders:** It's one of those things where you're like, "When am I ever going to be in a 17-play drive?" You might never see it. But you might see a 10-play drive. If you're ready for another seven more plays, that's why you do it.

**Justin Reid:** By the time you're done running the play, the next ball is already spotted.

**Trey Smith, right guard (third tour):** That's where, in my mind, I go into a different place and try to get to know myself. I know it sounds crazy, just verbalizing it. It differentiates yourself, especially at the end of the season. You have to really find who you are as a man.

**DeVito:** You have to get into that almost zombie mood where you're just trying to survive. Those shared experiences, when you're suffering together, is why you go away for camp.

**Donovan:** I was on the sideline last year. Those receivers get completely gassed. Marquez (Valdes-Scantling) came to the sideline and went down.

**Valdes-Scantling:** I was frustrated, like, "Why are we doing this stupid sh–?"

**Donovan:** (Former receiver) Mecole (Hardman) went up to him and goes, "Dude, I know what you're feeling! You have to get up! You have to do this!" I was like, "Damn!"

**George Karlaftis, defensive end (second tour):** You feel prepared for that first game.

**Trent McDuffie, cornerback (second tour):** Being in an uncomfortable state of mind really helps you, especially at the end of the season when you are tired and it's cold.

**Mahomes:** You're thinking the entire time. That puts

RIGHT: Chiefs fans flock to watch their favorite players at training camp in August.

as much stress on you as the physical toll. He wants to make sure you're paying attention to the littlest details. He'll ask you: "What's the down and distance on that last play?" You're like, "Man, we've ran eight plays in a row; I don't know." It's like second-and-7, and you're not even thinking about it. You're thinking about the play and getting everybody lined up. He'll ask you: 'How much time was left on the play clock before you snapped it?" He wants to make sure you're seeing everything the entire time, so when you get to the game, it's easy.

**Keondre Coburn, defensive tackle (first tour):** It's training your mindset to be ready at any moment because you never know what's going to happen in a game, (when) you won't be able to get a sub — and you got to play. I love it. I see why they've (the Chiefs) been great all these years.

**Valdes-Scantling:** We're in the Chargers game (November 2022), and we've got to go 75 yards (in the final two minutes) and score a touchdown. We go down the field (in just six plays) to win the game. Those are the type of moments that the long-drive drill prepares you for.

**Tranquill:** There's something in us, as human beings, when we do hard things and put that in our reservoir. It's about building this foundation so that when we're in Jacksonville in Week 2, and it's 90 degrees and 80 percent humidity, we're able to draw from that well of difficult circumstances.

**Saunders:** Against the Titans (November 2022), when we got into overtime, I felt about as fresh as I could. I got a couple stops on Derrick Henry and got a sack. That was probably my best game. That was a time when I was like, "Wow, I'm not tired."

**Schwartz:** When you see that backup defensive tackle — who, you're like, "Damn, I really like this guy; he's awesome, he gives me good looks and we have a good rapport" — gets in on a critical third down in a game and he gets a sack, you're more pumped than you ordinarily would be because you have this cool relationship of having gone (against one another) so much in camp.

*In a growing trend, 27 teams have scheduled joint practices with another team this year. Thirteen will practice against multiple opponents. Under Reid, the Chiefs have never participated in a joint practice.*

**Saunders:** We're just hitting each other for two-and-a-half weeks.

**Schwartz:** Coaches like it because they think it breaks up the monotony of camp and leads to a different level of emotional state. Most players will tell

**LEFT:** Chiefs players run drills on the first day of camp in St. Joseph.

you they hate joint practices. (Reid) trusts us to do the work against each other.

***

**Valdes-Scantling:** The hardest part, obviously, is sleeping in a dorm room when you've got a Sleep Number bed at home.

**James:** It makes you uncomfortable. You're sleeping in a twin bed.

**Schwartz:** They keep the dorms exceptionally cold. That's one thing you have to tell the young guys: Bring an extra blanket, which sounds crazy. But it gets frigid in there.

**Tom Melvin, tight ends coach (25th tour):** (Reid) is somebody who can survive on not a lot of sleep. I can't do that.

**Toub:** I hate the dorms. I'm 61 years old living in a concrete block.

**Saunders:** It definitely brings you back to that college feel. For what (Reid) does and what he's trying to accomplish, it's definitely more beneficial to where you can only focus on football.

**Schwartz:** (Reid) would say, "We want you guys to hang out as much as possible." You have enough time to hang out with your buddies, whether it's in your room playing video games, in the meal hall or hanging out after meetings.

**Saunders:** Me and (former safety) Tyrann Mathieu were just talking about that the other day. I've got some unreleased Tyrann Mathieu music on my laptop. I make music and people used to come to my dorm all the time and record stuff until curfew.

**Justin Reid:** It's fun playing chess with (guard) Joe Thuney. We've got a champion in Drue. I'm going to go challenge him and see if I can take the belt.

**Saunders:** I like to make all my teammates my friends, even O-linemen. We go against each other every day, but one of my closest friends is (guard Nick) Allegretti, just the camaraderie. That's probably my favorite part about the Chiefs' camp.

**Justin Reid:** I know a lot more guys (personally) on this team, from being here in St. Joe than I did in Houston just because you spend so much time together. There's a rock-paper-scissors competition going around the locker room.

**DeVito:** A lot of teams will break camp after the first preseason game. You get the taste of freedom. But Andy brings you back. That, hands down, is the most difficult part. Five more days of suffering.

**LEFT:** Chiefs training camp has a reputation for being the toughest in the league.

**Brett Veach, general manager (16th tour):** That's the beauty of Coach. Most guys are like, "Camp is over; we just played a game." Then Coach kicks them in the ass because that's what they're going to experience at some point.

**Schwartz:** Uh ... the favorite moment of camp is when you pack up and leave. No one truly enjoys camp.

**DeVito:** When do you feel comfortable in camp? When that b— is over. That's the only time.

**Toub:** He loves it. He's not going anywhere. People keep talking about retirement. He loves this. This is his hobby. I do other things. I like to play golf, go fishing. I'm trying to get him to go hunt. He won't do it. This is all he does: football.

**Mahomes:** I've told guys if you can get through Andy Reid's camp, then you're going to be able to get through an NFL season.

**DeVito:** They have that sign on the wall: Come in as a team, leave as a family. For a lot of teams, that would just be a motto. For Kansas City, that's real. When I think of those guys that I played with, I love those guys. I hadn't experienced anything like that. I really believe a major part of that is through the relationships you build during camp. The locker room was our fraternity. That's hard to do in the NFL, and that's what I miss the most. ∎

# Dropping the Ball

How the Receivers' Mistakes Cost Kansas City on Opening Night

BY NATE TAYLOR

They didn't expect to feel this way. This was supposed to be another celebration of their continued excellence. On another national TV stage, this time on the NFL's opening night, they would show they still have all the important people necessary — a future Hall of Fame coach, the sport's best quarterback and a talented young supporting cast — to remain the league's No. 1 team.

Yet the Kansas City Chiefs left their quiet locker room late Thursday night disappointed in themselves.

The scoreboards at Arrowhead Stadium displayed the league's first result of the 2023 season: Detroit Lions 21, Chiefs 20.

For the first time in his seven-year career, quarterback Patrick Mahomes experienced what it's like to lose the season's first game. Playing without All-Pro tight end Travis Kelce and All-Pro defensive tackle Chris Jones, the Chiefs had their eight-year streak of starting the season with a victory snapped. They had averaged 36.3 points in those games.

"Anytime I lose, I'm embarrassed," Mahomes said. "We've got to be better."

Mahomes completed 21 of 39 passes for 226 yards and two touchdowns. He also led his team in rushing, carrying six times for 45 yards. But the game's most important statistic wasn't included in the traditional box score: The Chiefs dropped eight of Mahomes' passes.

"They know I'm going to keep firing it, so we'll try to get it fixed this next week," Mahomes said, trying not to criticize his teammates. "It'll be good for the young guys to know that we're not just going to walk in and win the game."

Three of the Chiefs' final four possessions were sabotaged by a skill-position player dropping a catchable pass from Mahomes. Running back Jerick McKinnon, a 10-year veteran who made one of the mistakes, said he and his teammates — receivers Kadarius Toney, Skyy Moore and rookie Rashee Rice — were trying too hard to make a highlight in the open field before securing the ball.

"You can't make a play first unless you catch the ball," McKinnon said. "We had a lot of missed opportunities. We didn't make enough plays and we put our defense in a lot of bad positions. This one should hurt. It's a long season, but this (was) not our expectations."

The game's turning point came early in the third quarter when Mahomes threw a perfect pass to Toney, who was running a crossing route. Instead of catching the ball, Toney let it go through his hands and right to Lions rookie safety Brian Branch, who returned the interception 50 yards for a touchdown to tie the game 14-14. The Lions' win probability increased from 16 percent to 39 percent as a result, according to Next Gen Stats.

Toney, the Chiefs' projected No. 1 wide receiver, never got into sync with Mahomes. A three-year veteran, Toney missed training camp and the preseason while recovering from surgery to repair meniscus and cartilage in his knee. When Toney watched Branch enter the end zone with the ball that was intended for him, he bowed his head and shouted an expletive. Later in the third quarter, Toney dropped another pass while running a crossing route, an unforced error that stalled the Chiefs' drive in the red zone, forcing coach Andy Reid to use kicker Harrison Butker for a short field goal.

But Toney's most egregious drop came during the Chiefs' final dive. Trailing by one point with less than three minutes left, the Chiefs had the perfect play called against the Lions' zone coverage. Running a deep over route, Toney was wide open for what would've been at least a 25-yard completion, a connection that would've put the Chiefs close to Butker's range for a game-winning field goal. After the play, with fans booing Toney, Mahomes put his hands on his helmet in frustration.

"I have trust in KT," Mahomes said of Toney, who didn't speak with reporters. "Obviously, he wanted to play and he fought and rehabbed hard so he could play. Stuff is not always going to go your way. But I have trust that he's going to be that guy that I go to in those crucial moments and he's going to make the catch."

Kelce, who missed the game because of a hyperextended knee, a non-contact injury that occurred in Tuesday's practice, spent several minutes inside the locker room encouraging many of his offensive teammates in one-on-one conversations.

"The guy is a warrior," receiver Justin Watson said of Kelce. "He would do anything to play. I know he's

RIGHT: Detroit Lions players make a tackle on wide receiver Richie James during the Kansas City Chiefs' loss in Week 1.

going to be good. It's a long season and Travis is going to (be an) All-Pro. He's a huge part of our offense. We definitely missed Travis."

Without Kelce, the Lions were able to effectively guard most of the Chiefs' pass catchers with man-to-man coverage, especially after halftime.

"You're losing the best, I think, tight end of all time," Mahomes said. "But other guys have to step up."

About 30 minutes before kickoff, All-Pro defensive tackle Chris Jones, who is holding out for a lucrative contract extension, entered Arrowhead. None of Jones' attire featured red or gold colors. Sitting in a suite between his two agents, Jason Katz and Michael Katz, Jones watched his defensive teammates play well.

Coordinator Steve Spagnuolo called a plethora of blitzes that helped generate pressure on Lions quarterback Jared Goff. Cornerback Trent McDuffie forced a fumble, defensive end Mike Danna recorded a sack and safety Justin Reid made a leaping pass deflection near the line of scrimmage just before the two-minute warning to give the Chiefs offense one more chance. The Chiefs don't know when Jones will end his holdout, which could last until Week 8. But their defense held the Lions offense to 14 points.

"That wasn't even in my mind," Justin Reid said of Jones' absence. "I don't think that was in anyone's mind in the locker room. We're here to play a game and we didn't play (well) enough. You can't make any excuses about it. You have to come back and play better."

Before Thursday, the Chiefs were 22-18 in regular-season games when trailing in the second half since 2018, Mahomes' first year as a starter, the lone team with a winning record in that scenario during that stretch. The Chiefs believe they should've earned another thrilling comeback win Thursday.

But many of the Chiefs — including Mahomes, McKinnon and Watson — left Arrowhead knowing the biggest reason for their loss will be clear to see in their upcoming film session.

"Anytime the defense doesn't have to stop you," Watson said, "you stop yourself." ∎

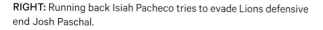

**RIGHT:** Running back Isiah Pacheco tries to evade Lions defensive end Josh Paschal.

# Back in the Fold

Chris Jones Bets on Himself with 1-Year Deal

BY NATE TAYLOR ———————— SEPTEMBER 13, 2023

The financial compromise that Chris Jones and the Kansas City Chiefs reached Monday afternoon was one that neither party anticipated making when negotiations began.

In June, the Chiefs were confident they were going to sign Jones, their star defensive tackle, to a multiyear extension. Jones, meanwhile, was confident he did plenty during the 2022 championship season to earn a lucrative extension, one that would make him the NFL's second-highest-paid defensive tackle by a wide margin.

Both parties believed they had proper leverage in the negotiations, too. The Chiefs felt they could secure Jones with a combination of guaranteed money and a continued place as an essential member — along with quarterback Patrick Mahomes and tight end Travis Kelce — of a perennial Super Bowl contender. Jones, 29, viewed himself as the league's most impactful pass rusher last season and knew the Chiefs built their entire defensive scheme around him.

Friction grew over the past seven weeks as Jones stayed away from the team, accruing daily fines.

On Monday, the parties reached an unexpected conclusion that solved their short-term issues but not their long-term goals. Jones signed a new one-year deal, replacing the final year of the four-year contract he signed in 2020. His base salary remained the same at $19.5 million, but he can earn a maximum of $25 million through incentives.

"Chris is an elite player in this league, and over the last seven years, he's really developed into a leader on our team," general manager Brett Veach said Monday in a statement. "He's been instrumental to our success and Super Bowl championship runs and it was a priority for us to keep him in a Chiefs uniform."

Three hours after Veach's statement, Jones expressed his enthusiasm through his X account, formerly Twitter.

"Letsssss gooooooooooo," Jones wrote Monday night.

Jones accrued $2.25 million in fines for the 45 days he missed, from July 21 to Sept. 3. He forfeited a workout bonus of $500,000 before training camp for not participating in the Chiefs' offseason program and was fined $98,573 for missing the team's mandatory minicamp. By skipping the Chiefs' season opener against the Detroit Lions, he forfeited his weekly game check of $1,083,333.

Jones, though, believes he can earn back that money — a total of $3.931 million — by achieving the incentives in his new contract.

Jones will earn $2 million if he plays at least 50 percent of the Chiefs' defensive snaps, according to a league source. If he collects 15 sacks, he will earn another $1.75 million. And Jones can earn another $1 million if he's a first-team All-Pro and the Chiefs reach the Super Bowl. He would receive an additional $2 million if the Chiefs win the Super Bowl and he wins the Defensive Player of the Year Award, which he has yet to accomplish in his eight-year career.

"It's a bunch of high-end honors, tied to the club's success, that (the Chiefs) will be happy to pay," said The Athletic's Randy Mueller, the former general manager of the Miami Dolphins and New Orleans Saints. "They'll be ecstatic to pay that money. They'll be having another parade.

"I don't know what (Jones) got out of this, other than less money."

Mueller believes Jones' leverage was at its peak last week before the Chiefs hosted the Lions. The day before the game, Jones made an appearance at Ronald McDonald House Charities of Kansas City as part of the Chiefs' annual Red Wednesday fundraising activities. Jones said multiple times that he was asking for a raise, an extension that would pay him an average annual salary of $30 million. Such an extension would've made Jones the league's third-highest-paid defensive player behind San Francisco 49ers pass rusher Nick Bosa, who agreed to a five-year, $170 million contract extension with $122.5 million guaranteed Wednesday, and Los Angeles Rams defensive tackle Aaron Donald.

The next day, Jones watched from an Arrowhead Stadium suite as the Chiefs lost 21-20 to the Lions. He stayed in Kansas City last weekend and the negotiations between the parties started intensifying Sunday, according to another league source.

"This is just a confirmation of what we already

**RIGHT:** After missing training camp and the season opener, Chris Jones rejoined the Chiefs for their 17-9 win over the Jaguars in Week 2.

know: These holdouts are disastrous," said Mueller, who co-hosts "The Football GM" podcast with The Athletic's Mike Sando. "They end with regret. It doesn't make sense to me. Sometimes agendas get involved that push you to do things that don't make any sense on the business side. You can't tell me this is right for the player."

Jones led the Chiefs in sacks and quarterback hits last season, matching his career highs of 15 1/2 and 29. He played 916 snaps — 80 percent of the unit's total — the most among Chiefs defensive linemen. He chose to hold out understanding this year could be his best opportunity to maximize his earning potential.

The Chiefs, who were determined to have Jones in uniform against the Lions, offered him a two-year, fully guaranteed extension worth $54.5 million, which would pay him an average annual salary of $27.5 million in 2024 and 2025, according to a league source. Jones declined the offer. Mueller believes the Chiefs' offer was fair.

"You saw (Monday) night what can happen," Mueller said of New York Jets quarterback Aaron Rodgers' tearing his Achilles tendon on just the fourth snap of the season. "The player's health is always at risk. It's tough. You never know. So am I willing to bet $50 million on that? No. I'm taking the $50 million."

Jones' future remains uncertain beyond this season. He is set to become a free agent after next spring, but the Chiefs could still place the franchise tag on him again in March, which would prevent him from reaching free agency while extending their time to negotiate an extension. If both parties cannot agree to an extension before the league's deadline for franchise-tagged players, Jones would be restricted to a one-year salary of $30.55 million, according to Over the Cap.

Another option for the Chiefs would be to use the franchise tag to help swing a trade for multiple picks before the draft.

"I'm not even considering trading him," Mueller said, putting himself in Veach's shoes. "I want to tag him to have him. If that's the way (Jones) wants his money paid to him, fine, that's a better deal than what (the Chiefs) offered him. It's better for the team because it doesn't come with a signing bonus or any structure that the player wants. It helps the team cash-flow wise."

Entering Tuesday, the Chiefs had just $681,069 in salary-cap space, the lowest amount in the league, according to Over the Cap.

Earlier this month, the Chiefs hoped signing Jones to an extension would create additional salary-cap space — perhaps as much as $12 million — for them to sign another veteran defensive lineman to help the pass rush. Since Jones' new contract didn't accomplish that goal, the Chiefs restructured star left guard Joe Thuney's contract, a move that created $8.7 million in salary-cap space.

If Jones has another excellent season, Mueller said he and his agents could approach Veach in December or January to see whether the Chiefs want to restart talks on a multiyear extension. Such a decision, Mueller said, would further prove Jones intends to play his entire career in Kansas City.

"I would probably make them come to me with something that they would sign," Mueller said if he were Veach. "(The Chiefs) have already danced and done this dog-and-pony show for three months." ∎

---

**LEFT:** After prolonged negotiations, Chris Jones agreed to a contract with numerous incentives for achievements such as reaching the Super Bowl.

# Blowout

### Chiefs 'Get the Whole Offense Going' Against Bears

———————— BY NATE TAYLOR

Some days are perfect. Sunday's game for the Kansas City Chiefs was one of them. The NFL loves to boast about its parity, its idea that every week is a challenge for every team and its love of the phrase, "any given Sunday."

The Chiefs, though, were given a gift on their schedule: The floundering Chicago Bears.

The weather was perfect, too, a sunny 82-degree afternoon at kickoff. The Arrowhead Stadium atmosphere is as close as the league comes to that of an important college football game, thousands of fans tailgating with the biggest sensory accent being the smell of barbecue. In a rare occurrence, Sunday's game resembled a college homecoming, the Bears being the perfect overmatched opponent for the Chiefs to put up their first complete, dominating performance of the season.

The Chiefs' 41-10 victory — in which they scored the first 41 points — was the ideal game for their offense to fully awaken and show its full capabilities.

"It feels good to get the whole offense going," quarterback Patrick Mahomes said. "I was proud of the guys."

Entering the game, the Chiefs and the Bears averaged the same number of points per game: 18.5.

Almost every aspect of the Chiefs offense Sunday was better than their two previous games when the unit struggled with dropped passes, penalties and turnovers. But against the Bears' beleaguered defense, the Chiefs offense scored on seven consecutive possessions, scoring a touchdown on each of five trips inside the red zone. The Chiefs averaged 7 yards per play before halftime.

"The first two weeks, we didn't look too sharp," running back Jerick McKinnon said. "We got challenged by the coaches. We challenged ourselves and we came out and got off on the right track."

One of the best adjustments from coach Andy Reid and offensive coordinator Matt Nagy was to involve the Chiefs' running backs early. A week earlier, in a win over the Jacksonville Jaguars, Reid and Nagy called just two designed running plays for McKinnon and Isiah Pacheco. With 32 total rushing attempts, the Chiefs' trio of running backs — McKinnon, Pacheco and Clyde Edwards-Helaire — produced 125 yards and four touchdowns.

"For how teams are playing us with those zone coverages, we're going to have to run the ball," Mahomes said. "Getting those guys going downhill, it opens everything else. When the run game gets going, that's when the offense gets going."

Seven of Mahomes' 24 completions went to the running backs for a total of 37 yards and two touchdowns, both by McKinnon.

"We said it all week: We're trying to go for a hat trick," McKinnon said of each running back reaching the end zone. "We just maximized the opportunity."

Mahomes, who was rarely pressured, finished with 272 passing yards, three touchdowns and no interceptions for a 127.3 rating. Early in the third quarter, Mahomes became the fastest player in league history to reach 25,000 career passing yards, accomplishing the feat in just 83 games (Los Angeles Rams quarterback Matthew Stafford previously held the record, doing so in 90 games).

Mahomes' best completion came midway through the second quarter when he moved up in the pocket and jumped to deliver an impressive 37-yard strike to receiver Justin Watson.

"It was a heck of a way of tracking the ball, staying in bounds and making a tough catch," Mahomes said of Watson. "I have a lot of confidence in (Watson), and he makes a lot of plays."

But it wasn't Watson or the speedy Marquez Valdes-Scantling who led the Chiefs in receiving yards. Instead, rookie Rashee Rice had five receptions for 59 yards, leading the team with 31 yards after the catch to combat the Bears' soft zone coverage. Twice inside the red zone, Mahomes trusted Rice in the middle of the field, a positive sign of the rookie's progress within the Chiefs offense.

"They brought a new safety in and I was like, 'Hey, they're probably going to be in Cover 2, so it's going to be your ball,'" Valdes-Scantling said of Rice. "He didn't even realize it. Then, they go Cover 2, he catches the ball and splits the safeties and almost scores a touchdown. I'm glad I can be in this role to teach him things that I know.

"The defense is playing lights out, so it was only a matter of time before we figured it out. This is a step in

**RIGHT:** Patrick Mahomes threw for 272 yards and three touchdowns against the Chicago Bears.

the right direction of what we can do and what we're expecting ourselves to do."

The lone issue for the Chiefs was that Mahomes suffered a minor right ankle injury, the same ankle he injured in January. On a routine dropback, Mahomes delivered a short pass to receiver Watson but was rolled up from behind by defensive end Yannick Ngakoue, who fell to the turf after being blocked by left tackle Donovan Smith.

After the play, Mahomes grimaced while hobbling. Although he limped between plays, he finished the drive to end the half, then returned to the field to start the third quarter, leading the Chiefs to their final touchdown on an 11-play, 64-yard drive.

"It would've been fine to play the rest of the game," said Mahomes, who was replaced by backup Blaine Gabbert late in the third quarter. "If anything, it kind of scared me more, just being that ankle."

Once Mahomes showed he wasn't seriously injured, the game's most interesting subplot, with the outcome already determined, was whether he and tight end Travis Kelce were going to connect for a touchdown.

In an unusual scenario, Mahomes wasn't the most famous person at Arrowhead. Pop superstar Taylor Swift was in a suite sitting next to Kelce's mother, Donna.

Wearing a white T-shirt, a Chiefs jacket and her signature red lipstick, Swift cheered for the home team, creating a massive amount of hoopla because of rumors she and Kelce are dating. Mahomes' final pass, a 3-yard connection to Kelce in the back of the end zone, led to Swift's celebrating by jumping, applauding and shouting three words: "Let's freaking go!"

After the victory, Kelce exited Arrowhead alongside Swift as if they were the homecoming king and queen, the couple riding toward downtown in his burgundy convertible.

"She's a tremendous singer," Mahomes said. "I haven't gotten to meet her. But I guess if she ends up being with Travis, then I'll probably get to meet her at some point. She seems like a good person, so hopefully I get to meet her one day." ■

**RIGHT:** Tight end Travis Kelce and running back Jerick McKinnon celebrate after a touchdown.

# 'All Heart'

### Kelce Wills Chiefs to Victory Over Vikings

——————— BY NATE TAYLOR

Surrounded by Kansas City Chiefs teammates, Travis Kelce stood in the corner of the visitors locker room inside US Bank Stadium on Sunday, his smile growing wider and wider the more he heard them talk about him.

Receiver Marquez Valdes-Scantling thought Kelce had torn his Achilles tendon, an injury that would've ended the season for the Chiefs' No.1 pass catcher. Receiver Skyy Moore made a joke, one he knew would make Kelce laugh: He suggested that the NFL's best tight end somehow found a new way to clumsily injure himself. When it looked like the Chiefs would have to play the second half against the Minnesota Vikings without Kelce, the receivers were surprised to learn that the coaches planned to use receiver Justin Watson at tight end on some plays.

Kelce kept smiling. He could relish his teammates' enthusiasm in the immediate aftermath of the Chiefs' 27-20 victory because he pulled off one of the most heroic performances of his 11-year career.

With each snap Kelce played in the second half, he felt pain in his lower right leg because of a low-ankle sprain, a non-contact injury that occurred during the Chiefs' two-minute drill before halftime. Despite the injury, Kelce's performance didn't suffer. He summoned the strength and determination to produce vintage reception after vintage reception, to help the Chiefs win their fourth consecutive game.

Kelce finished with 10 receptions on 11 targets for a team-leading 67 yards, including the winning touchdown. On their way to the showers, many of the Chiefs gave Kelce a high-five or a quick handshake.

"That was a team win," Kelce said repeatedly to his teammates.

In a short exchange with The Athletic, Kelce explained that Sunday's injury was similar to his first injury of the season when he hyperextended his right knee in the final practice before the season opener. A month ago, Kelce planted his right foot while running a route, a non-contact injury that forced him to miss a game for the first time since 2014. Without Kelce, the Chiefs lost 21-20 to the Detroit Lions.

Late in the second quarter Sunday, the Chiefs were trailing the Vikings by three points when quarterback Patrick Mahomes completed a short pass to Kelce. Once again, Kelce planted his right foot and slipped, this time

on slit-film turf, which NFL and NFLPA data shows has had a higher rate of non-contact lower extremity injuries than other types of artificial turf. Instead of changing directions in the open field, Kelce rolled his ankle. He hobbled off the field and went to the locker room just minutes before kicker Harrison Butker made a 40-yard field goal to end the second quarter.

"I don't like to talk to Travis when he's hurting because he's a mean guy," Mahomes said, smiling. "I kind of just peeked in and looked at (head athletic trainer) Rick (Burkholder) and just asked, 'How are we feeling?'"

Burkholder, while taping up Kelce's right cleat, said: "He's going to try and see if he can go."

Kelce was the last Chief to return to the field for the second half. He jogged to the sideline in an attempt to inspire his teammates. The moment was also the first test for Kelce, who was trying to gauge if he could tolerate the pain.

Kelce told coach Andy Reid that the team's medical staff cleared him to return.

"He said, 'Just give me a minute; I'm going to get this thing right,'" Reid said of Kelce. "He did a bunch of drills on his own."

With Kelce watching from the sideline, the Chiefs anticipated that the Vikings, the league's most blitz-happy defense through four weeks, would increase their five- and six-man pressures. The game's first pivotal play came early in the third quarter on a third-and-18 snap. The Vikings sent seven defenders at Mahomes. Similar to his game-changing 44-yard completion in the fourth quarter of the Chiefs' comeback win in Super Bowl LIV, Mahomes backpedaled 7 yards from the shotgun after the snap to create enough time to unleash a deep pass toward Watson, who was running a deep over route.

"I didn't necessarily see it, but I put it up there for J-Wat," Mahomes said. "He made a play for me."

Vikings safety Camryn Bynum could've intercepted the pass but mistimed his jump. Watson leaped at the right moment for a 33-yard reception.

"Take the elevator up to the penthouse, not everybody's access card swipes that high," Watson said,

**RIGHT:** Despite an injury during the second quarter, Travis Kelce managed 10 receptions for 67 yards.

smiling. "We were just talking vertical jumps this week in the receivers room. Some guys were talking about who had the highest vert. My name wasn't mentioned. I was glad to get that one on film.

"Coach Reid always says that we're trying to rip their hearts out. They're thinking they're getting off the field and it's awesome coming up with a play that tells them we're keeping this drive going."

The Vikings kept blitzing on the drive — and Mahomes kept burning them with completions. He generated 66 passing yards on the drive, connecting with Watson, Valdes-Scantling and receivers Justyn Ross and Rashee Rice. Mahomes ended the drive with a perfect 8-yard touchdown pass to Rice. The first Chief to congratulate Mahomes and Rice was Kelce.

"That was a great f—— drive," Kelce said.

Kelce returned to the field on the Chiefs' next possession. The drive's third snap ended with Kelce's most impressive reception of the game. Against tight coverage from safety Josh Metellus, Kelce leaped, caught the ball with Metellus' right arm between his hands and squeezed the ball tight enough to maintain possession while crashing to the turf for a 14-yard gain.

"I feel like Travis has the same mindset as I do," Mahomes said. "If you give him the window (so) he can get back in the game, he's going to be back in the game. He's a competitor, man. That's why he's one of the greatest."

Six plays later, the Chiefs faced a third-and-8 inside the red zone and called a play with Kelce intended to be a decoy. Mahomes pump-faked a quick pass to Kelce, hoping that receiver Kadarius Toney would be open on a wheel route in the corner of the end zone. But with the Vikings in zone coverage, rookie cornerback Mekhi Blackmon stayed with Toney. Mahomes began scrambling, unsure what he would do to get the first down.

"I stepped up in the pocket and Travis is supposed to be (near) the sideline," Mahomes said. "Luckily, he was running across the field. I have those moments where I go, 'Ah... I'm about to get crushed.' Then I look over and (No.) 87 is just running free. He's been with me a long time and knows how to get himself open."

With their improvisation in sync, Mahomes and Kelce connected on a short pass that resulted in an 11-yard gain. Two plays later, the Vikings stayed in zone coverage and the Chiefs called a perfect play. Kelce changed directions, going from right to left, to run a short comeback route behind Valdes-Scantling and Watson to get wide open for an easy 4-yard touchdown catch.

"He finds a new way to surprise me every week," Watson said of Kelce. "That looked like a gnarly injury. I was surprised that he even made it off the sideline. ... He fired us all up coming back in there and making some plays."

Mahomes celebrated the score by sprinting to Kelce for a face mask-to-face mask celebration.

"Let's go!" Kelce shouted to Mahomes.

On the game's final play, Kelce was in the end zone, the lone offensive player to join the Chiefs defense to help prevent Vikings quarterback Kirk Cousins from completing a 38-yard Hail Mary touchdown pass. Kelce, though, never needed to jump for the ball. Defensive end Mike Danna ended the game by sacking Cousins.

Leaving the field, Kelce became emotional when he looked into the stands and saw Chiefs cheering for him. Kelce pointed to his chest.

"All heart, baby!" he shouted. "All heart, baby!"

Kelce was one of the final Chiefs to leave the locker room for the team bus. Limping slightly, he spent several minutes in the training room. Before that, though, Kelce told The Athletic that he intends to be with his teammates on the field Thursday night when the Chiefs host the Denver Broncos in the team's shortest turnaround between games this season.

"I know what I have to do," Kelce said. "I have to accept the challenge, baby!" ■

---

**LEFT:** Travis Kelce celebrates with offensive tackle Jawaan Taylor as the Chiefs defeated the Vikings.

# Best of the West

## Chiefs in Total Control of Their Division and Only Getting Better

BY NATE TAYLOR

For almost a decade, their divisional rivals have schemed, plotted and made changes — at head coach, quarterback and other positions — to put an end to their dominance.

The Kansas City Chiefs, though, keep thwarting their AFC West foes — the Los Angeles Chargers, the Denver Broncos and the Las Vegas Raiders — by continuing to win. And win. And win.

Sunday's battle between the Chiefs and the Chargers was the latest example, an outcome that felt familiar for both teams: a Chiefs' 31-17 victory.

Even with a defensive-minded coach (Brandon Staley), a star quarterback (Justin Herbert) and several above-average defenders (pass rushers Khalil Mack and Joey Bosa and safety Derwin James Jr.), the Chargers never led.

Even when the Chargers devoted several defenders to disrupt the connection between the superstar duo of quarterback Patrick Mahomes and tight end Travis Kelce, the pair generated 12 completions on 13 targets for 179 yards.

Even though most analysts pegged the Chargers as the Chiefs' biggest threat, the AFC West is not a tight race after seven weeks.

"These games count twice," safety Justin Reid said of the Chiefs winning 39 of their last 44 divisional games. "We know how big of a deal this is for other teams and for us. You want to win your division first."

No team is closer to winning its division in the NFL than the Chiefs (6-1), who widened the gap between them and created an even wider gap Sunday between themselves and the Raiders (3-4), the Chargers (2-4) and the Broncos (2-5).

The Chiefs are alone atop the conference and — here's a scary thought for the rest of the AFC — they're only getting better.

"We're definitely taking steps in the right direction," Mahomes said of the Chiefs offense.

Mahomes enjoyed his best performance of the season, throwing for a season-high 424 yards and four touchdowns. Within the pocket, Mahomes' accuracy and decisions were exquisite as he completed at least one pass to 10 teammates. His first highlight included improvisation as he scrambled to his right to find speedy receiver Marquez Valdes-Scantling for a 46-yard touchdown.

When the Chargers blitzed, Mahomes often scrambled for a first down or threw a completion — usually to Kelce — to keep the Chiefs moving downfield. The Chargers' secondary spent much of the first half in zone coverage. Mahomes responded by targeting Kelce in the middle of the field nine times. Each target was a completion as Kelce produced 143 yards before halftime.

"The main thing is the way he's able to recognize coverage and adjust on the fly," Mahomes said of Kelce. "It's almost like he's playing 'Madden,' like he can read the coverages and stop in the (zone) windows and be open and be on the same page as me at all times. He did a great job. He'll be a Hall of Famer one day."

Mahomes' final completion of the half was to Kelce, who caught the ball behind the offensive line and was still able — with the ball above his helmet — to score a 1-yard touchdown.

"Kelce keeps getting better with time, and Taylor can stay around all she wants," coach Andy Reid said, referencing pop superstar Taylor Swift, who watched the game in a suite sitting next to Mahomes' wife, Brittany.

The Chargers kept pace with the Chiefs for the game's first 28 minutes. They used an up-tempo offense to prevent Chiefs defensive coordinator Steve Spagnuolo from rotating defenders. When the Chargers snapped the ball faster than usual, they had Herbert throw the ball deep. On another quick snap, the Chargers scored on a 49-yard rushing touchdown from running back Joshua Kelley, the longest gain the Chiefs have surrendered this season.

"They got us on a few," Reid said of the Chargers. "But the guys figured it out. The pressure on (Herbert), that was an unsettled position for him. Whether they were sacking him or hitting him, he had people around him all the time."

The Chiefs finished with a season-high five sacks, each from a different player not named Chris Jones. Defensive ends George Karlaftis, Mike Danna and Charles Omenihu and linebackers Willie Gay and Drue Tranquill took Herbert down.

**RIGHT:** Running back Isiah Pacheco celebrates with teammates after a touchdown catch.

In the second half, Herbert completed just seven of his 16 passes for 100 yards. The Chiefs shut out the Chargers in the second half and have yet to allow an opponent to score more than 21 points.

Omenihu was one of the unit's most impactful contributors. The free-agent acquisition played in his first game with the Chiefs after serving a six-game suspension for violating the league's personal conduct policy. He finished with a sack, two quarterback hits, a tackle for loss and a pivotal pass deflection near the line of scrimmage in the third quarter that led to an interception in the red zone for cornerback L'Jarius Sneed.

"He went crazy," Jones said of Omenihu. "If we continue to get that effort from Charles, we can be a dynamic defensive line."

Entering Sunday, the Chiefs ranked 25th in the league in TruMedia's special teams expected points added (STEPA), a metric used to gauge the scoreboard impact of special team plays. Receiver Mecole Hardman provided a much-needed spark for the return game with a 50-yard punt return in the fourth quarter.

Just four days earlier, the Chiefs acquired Hardman in a trade with the New York Jets, sending a 2025 sixth-round pick for a 2025 seventh-round pick. Later in the quarter, Hardman's first reception was a 6-yard gain that led to a first down inside the red zone. The Chiefs finished the drive with an 8-yard touchdown on a screen pass from Mahomes to running back Isiah Pacheco.

"I just wanted to give our team some momentum, man," Hardman said. "(Punter JK Scott) had been kicking it high and short the whole game. Finally, I saw a ball I could return. I made the most of it. Making an explosive play for the team means a lot."

Perhaps the most encouraging part of the Chiefs' improvement is their offense scored 31 points for the first time in almost a month and the unit finished with a touchdown in the fourth quarter without much of a contribution from Kelce.

Mahomes connected with a different teammate for each of his touchdowns — Kelce, Valdes-Scantling, Pacheco and rookie receiver Rashee Rice.

"Guys just stepped up," Mahomes said. "If they're going to focus that much on Travis, obviously we're going to still try to throw him the ball in certain areas, but other guys have to make plays. I think that's what our offense is going to continue to be." ■

**RIGHT:** Defensive end George Karlaftis hits Chargers quarterback Justin Herbert during Week 7.

# Travis Kelce

**What Makes Travis Kelce the NFL's Best Tight End**

BY NATE TAYLOR ——————— NOVEMBER 2, 2023

Once the game ended, the rookie approached the 11-year veteran, the two men not wearing the same uniform.

Scott Matlock, the defensive end for the Los Angeles Chargers, wanted to ask Travis Kelce, the superstar tight end for the Kansas City Chiefs, a question: Do you have any advice for a rookie? Kelce, a future Hall of Famer, responded by revealing a major component of his success.

"You know what it is?" Kelce said to Matlock. "Understand the other side of the ball just as well as you know your side of the ball. You feel me? Everything is predicated off of what I'm doing and what the defense is doing."

Kelce had just demonstrated that advice against the Chargers last month, his impressive performance a critical reason why the Chiefs were victorious. One of the Chargers' priorities against the Chiefs was to limit how many of quarterback Patrick Mahomes' passes Kelce caught. To that end, the Chargers' secondary played a variety of zone coverages. Still, Kelce finished with a game-high 12 receptions for 179 yards, including a touchdown.

Even though the Chargers at times assigned two defenders to cover Kelce, the tight end was able to thwart such a tactic, doing so to such a degree that it's understandable why fans, CBS play-by-play announcer Jim Nantz and even the Chargers themselves asked a similar version of the same question: How does Kelce consistently get open?

The answer is Kelce is capable of executing something daring that most tight ends or receivers cannot. He can recognize the opposing defense's coverage, alter his route — oftentimes deciding to run a completely different route in the middle of the play — and still be available and in rhythm with Mahomes before the ball is passed to him.

Early in the fourth quarter, on a second-and-10 snap, Kelce was supposed to run a 6-yard out route. But when he noticed that Chargers safety Derwin James played outside leverage, which could take away his initial route, Kelce changed directions, running a drag route. By running away from James, Kelce was able to make eye contact with Mahomes, who moved up in the pocket before the duo connected on a 14-yard completion.

"It's one thing when it goes right," Kelce said. "Then you want to do something based off of what you just did, knowing that the defense saw it. It's nonstop playing chess with the guys across from you.

"You've just got to make sure you're on the same page and you're not putting the team in a tough spot or putting Pat in a tough spot."

Earlier in the game, Kelce ran a route that no coach would draw on their whiteboard. With the Chargers in zone coverage, Kelce ran a short dig route before quickly turning upfield — to get behind James and linebacker Eric Kendricks — before turning his body back to Mahomes, who was moving up in the pocket. Mahomes lofted the ball over four defenders to Kelce for a 28-yard gain.

"Don't know why," Mahomes said. "I just kind of understand when he's going to do some stuff that he's not really supposed to do."

———————

One of Kelce's touchdowns this season happened because he improvised his route.

Near the goal line, the Chiefs started their third-and-goal play against the Chicago Bears with Kelce in a bunch formation next to tight end Noah Gray and receiver Marquez Valdes-Scantling. When Kelce heard the play call from Mahomes, his assignment was to run a corner route to the back pylon. But just before the ball was snapped, Kelce anticipated and visualized himself ending the play in the back of the end zone near the goal post. The Bears were in zone coverage, matching Kelce with safety Elijah Hicks. Kelce started his route running directly at Hicks, making the defender commit to covering the perimeter of the end zone. But after planting his right foot, Kelce ran a corner-post route, double move to create plenty of space for him to get open.

"In practice, where we were thinking about making a call for that, when we get that look for him to (change his route)," Mahomes said of Kelce. "I remember I was telling the coaches, 'I mean, I don't know why we need

**RIGHT:** Travis Kelce credits his understanding of opposing defenses for his success at tight end.

a call; he's going to do it anyways.' So of course he does it and it's a touchdown."

While the fans inside Arrowhead Stadium cheered Kelce's 3-yard touchdown reception, Mahomes could only smile.

"I'm glad you saw it," Mahomes said to Kelce when they celebrated. "I didn't know if you were going to do it."

On the sideline, Mahomes told some of his teammates, many of them on defense, that the reason the play worked was because Kelce did what he wanted to do.

"The crazy part is I knew he was going to do it," Mahomes said, laughing. "I was like, 'He ain't running a corner.' ... I was like, 'He's going to do it! He's going to do it! Ope, he did it.'"

--------

Although Kelce is the Chiefs' longest-tenured player, at age 34, he still wants as many repetitions as he can get during practice, whether in training camp or during the season.

Each rep is an opportunity for Kelce to experiment within the play's structure or the defense's coverage rules. A former quarterback in high school, Kelce has the rare ability to run his route — or change his mind with his route — and still visualize what the quarterback wants to see from him while in the pocket.

"He has a good understanding of the whole entire concept and he understands the coverages," Mahomes said of Kelce. "It takes a lot of reps. I'm just trying to develop that trust that whenever I'm seeing it one way, he's going to do it that way."

Coach Andy Reid, a former tight ends coach with the Green Bay Packers, realized that tight ends could be given more freedom in the West Coast offense because they run most of their routes from the middle of the field. Reid said former players — such as Keith Jackson, Mark Chmura, Chad Lewis and Brent Celek — were able to modify their routes depending on the defense's coverage and the offense's formation.

As Reid's offensive playbook has evolved over the years — incorporating the Air Raid, the pistol and old-school option offenses — Kelce has studied each variation of the Chiefs' passing concepts and has found the spaces, often in the short and intermediate areas of the field, where he can ad-lib without disrupting his teammates' routes.

LEFT: Travis Kelce celebrates after his touchdown catch during the AFC Championship game against the Baltimore Ravens.

"He does it better than anybody," Reid said of Kelce. "He's had a great feel right from the get-go. He's quarterback-friendly. He did it with (former quarterback) Alex (Smith), and he's done it now with Pat."

In 2018, when Mahomes became the Chiefs' starter, the teammate who was next to him the most, whether after reps in practice or on the sideline before the next drive, was Kelce. Midway through that season, Kelce began learning Mahomes' preferences when the quarterback scrambled out of the pocket to extend plays. Known for his creativity and improvisation skills, Mahomes learned to rely on Kelce for completions that resembled backyard football more than how the initial play was drawn.

"There's the first act: That's the pass on time," Denver Broncos coach Sean Payton said of Kelce and Mahomes. "Then, there's the brief intermission. Then we get to the second act: That's out of the pocket. They do that as well as anyone."

Entering Sunday's game against the Miami Dolphins in Frankfurt, Germany, Kelce leads all tight ends with 583 yards. If he records a touchdown reception, Kelce would tie Jason Witten for the fifth most (74) by a tight end in NFL history. Kelce also would become the fourth tight end to record at least five touchdown receptions in seven consecutive seasons, joining Antonio Gates, Hall of Famer Tony Gonzalez and Greg Olsen.

Together, Mahomes and Kelce have accounted for 50 touchdowns.

"It's like they're on the playground," said Jason Garrett, an NBC analyst and a former NFL quarterback and head coach. "Mahomes extends the play, Travis feels what he's seeing and they make connections. They do it week after week. They're simpatico."

In 2019, Mahomes started to anticipate when Kelce was going rogue with his routes, each of them breaking their usual tendencies to manipulate defenders to their advantage.

"Not only did I get a feel for how he runs routes, but he got a feel for how I was seeing stuff," Mahomes said. "We can kind of go off the radar screen and kind of develop some stuff that's not necessarily called."

One of Mahomes' favorite moments came during the 2019 postseason, which ended with the Chiefs going on to become Super Bowl LIV champions. In the middle of a play against the Houston Texans, Mahomes realized that Kelce was going to adjust his route before he actually made a cutback toward the middle of the field. Mahomes released the ball before Kelce turned back to make the reception, both players ad-libbing at the same time.

When the offense returned to the sideline after scoring a touchdown, Kelce approached Mahomes to ask a question: How did Mahomes know what his

teammate was doing at the exact moment as he was doing it?

"I really didn't," Mahomes said in 2020, looking back on the play. "I just *did* it. I just let it go. That's just the instincts that I have."

Kelce's most famous improvised route came in the final minute of regulation in the memorable 2021 divisional playoff game against the Buffalo Bills. With the Chiefs near midfield and trailing by three points, the Bills called a timeout after they saw the Chiefs' formation, which featured Kelce as the lone receiving option on the left side of the field. While the Bills discussed their defensive strategy, Kelce shared an idea with Mahomes, one of creativity and gumption. He told Mahomes he wanted to run a route he thought the Bills could never anticipate: a slick out-and-up route.

After the timeout, Mahomes watched the Bills' defense set up from the shotgun. Just one defender, between the line of scrimmage and 20 yards away, was on the left side of the field and in front of Kelce.

*"Do it, Kelce!" Mahomes shouted. "Do it! Do it, Kelce!"*

Lining up in the same spot, Kelce's nifty route started with him leaning to the left, which gave the impression he was heading toward the sideline, the exact area the one defender was most responsible for covering. But with his left foot, Kelce shifted his

body back forward before turning his head toward Mahomes, who delivered it to him in stride for a 25-yard reception that set up a game-tying field goal.

The Chiefs won the game in overtime when Mahomes threw a walk-off, game-winning 8-yard touchdown reception to Kelce, who beat linebacker Matt Milano on a smooth out-and-up route to the corner of the end zone.

"He's such a unique, fascinating, incredible player," Chiefs linebacker Drue Tranquill said of Kelce. "He's so unchoreographed in a lot of his movements. He'll stem you in and you're thinking, 'He's definitely going over.' Then, he's going back out. He's a rare combination of speed, size and strength. He's got a lot of finesse to his game that makes him really difficult to guard."

———

When he was younger, Kelce became the league's best tight end because of above-average speed and elite athleticism.

Now, as an 11-year veteran, Kelce has found different ways to maintain his status as No. 1. He has remained durable, his understanding of opposing defenses has never been better and his physical skills have yet to drastically decline, even though he is the same age as Rob Gronkowski, the future Hall of Famer who retired after the 2021 season.

"I believe that Travis Kelce is the best receiving tight end," Gronkowski said on "The Ryen Russillo Podcast" last month. "He's the best tight end (ever) in terms of catching the ball. There's no doubt about

**LEFT:** The partnership of Patrick Mahomes and Travis Kelce has been central to the Chiefs' championship success. **ABOVE:** Kelce's relationship with pop superstar Taylor Swift garnered attention throughout the season.

it. He's had seven 1,000-yard seasons in a row. He's a great red-zone target as well. When he's not out on the field with the Chiefs, which is very rare, they're not the same team."

By serving as the Chiefs' top pass catcher instead of a wide receiver, Kelce has become just the eighth tight end in league history to have at least 500 yards at age 34 or older.

"It's hard to find a guy this old where the second receiver (on the same team) is so far behind him," said Aaron Schatz, the chief analytics officer of FTN Network. "The big thing about Kelce is the amount of targets he gets compared to other tight ends is remarkable. In Weeks 1-5, he was targeted on 36 percent of his routes. No other tight end was above 30 percent. Receivers are usually not that high. He's very special. There's no other player like Kelce in the league right now."

Kelce is also exceptional when runs his intended route, which most often happens against man-to-man coverage.

Last season, Kelce burned Rams cornerback Jalen Ramsey on an option route in the middle of the field. At the top of his route, Kelce wiggled to the outside before changing directions to become wide open for a reception that ended in a 39-yard touchdown. Kelce made a similar move at the line of scrimmage last season when he beat James on a shallow route across the field for a game-winning 17-yard touchdown.

Last month in the Chiefs' win over the Broncos, Kelce altered his route by using a hesitation move against star cornerback Patrick Surtain II to create enough separation to catch a contested pass from Mahomes for a 19-yard gain. In the same game, Kelce changed his intermediate route as the play progressed against the Broncos' zone coverage, getting behind linebacker Josey Jewell for a 40-yard reception.

"He's super smart," Chiefs cornerback Trent Mc-Duffie said. "I've definitely seen a few moves he's pulled out on us (in camp) that he's used over the season. Once you're on the sideline and we're going against somebody else, you can really appreciate him."

By rarely running the same route identically in the same game — especially against zone coverage — Kelce has been able to generate 5,096 yards after the catch, the most by a tight end in league history.

Earlier this season, Mahomes and Kelce connected on 28 consecutive targets. The odds of the pair completing every one of the 28 targets, based on the completion probability of each attempt, was 0.03 percent

— the equivalent of one in 3,000 — according to Next Gen Stats.

"It's like he's mind-melded with Mahomes," Schatz said of Kelce.

The greatest example of their chemistry during the completion streak came in the Chiefs' win last month over the Minnesota Vikings.

Late in the third quarter, the Chiefs faced a third-and-8 inside the red zone and called a play with Kelce intended to be a decoy. Mahomes pump-faked a quick pass to Kelce, hoping that receiver Kadarius Toney would be open on a wheel route in the corner of the end zone. But with the Vikings in zone coverage, rookie cornerback Mekhi Blackmon stayed with Toney. Mahomes began scrambling, unsure what he would do to get the first down.

Kelce, though, matched Mahomes' ad-libbing with his own improvisation to reestablish eye contact with his quarterback. Mahomes released the ball and Kelce turned the short completion into an 11-yard gain. The highlight set up the Chiefs' game-winning touchdown, an easy 4-yard touchdown pass from Mahomes to Kelce.

"I stepped up in the pocket and Travis is supposed to be (near) the sideline," Mahomes said after the game. "Luckily, he was running across the field. I have those moments where I go, 'Ah ... I'm about to get crushed.' Then I look over and (No.) 87 is just running free. He's been with me a long time and knows how to get himself open." ∎

---

**LEFT:** Travis Kelce is interviewed ahead of Super Bowl LVIII in Las Vegas.

# 'How We Planned It'

## Chiefs Defense Steals the Show — And the Ball — In Germany

BY NATE TAYLOR

With each large stride he took near the sideline, Kansas City Chiefs safety Bryan Cook heard the diverse crowd roar, the volume rising and rising and rising as he sprinted toward his destination. The crescendo Cook heard matched the dazzling performance of the moment and the play's significance in the outcome of the NFL's first game in this city.

Cook held the ball in his left hand and raised his right to the crowd when he reached the end zone. The exhilarated crowd of 50,023 fans at Deutsche Bank Park — a gathering of Germans, Kansas Citians and other Europeans — saw Cook's gesture and were thrilled to grant his request: They produced an even louder ovation.

The best international matchup in NFL history — featuring two teams that entered four games over .500, the Chiefs and the Miami Dolphins — proved to be a showcase of one of the league's best defensive units.

Cook's touchdown before halftime was the difference-making highlight that propelled the Chiefs to an entertaining 21-14 victory.

The first teammate to celebrate with Cook, hugging him in the back of the end zone, was fellow safety Mike Edwards, whose selflessness and quick thinking sprung Cook on his way to the end zone. At the same time, in the middle of the field, quarterback Patrick Mahomes ran to dap another defensive teammate: cornerback Trent McDuffie, who ignited the takeaway.

The play took an unusual amount of time. The 14-second sequence consisted of three acts.

The Dolphins (6-3) had an opportunity to score their first points in the final minute of the second quarter. The play started with the Dolphins 30 yards from the end zone, as quarterback Tua Tagovailoa threw a short pass behind the line of scrimmage to receiver Tyreek Hill, who was playing against his former team for the first time. But McDuffie — the Chiefs' first-round draft pick in 2022 in the wake of the Hill trade to the Dolphins — recognized the play's design from his film study. McDuffie popped Hill less than a second after he caught the ball.

"When I made the hit, I definitely felt (the ball) get loose and tried my best to strip it out," said McDuffie, who leads the Chiefs with three forced fumbles.

Instead of recording a tackle for a loss, McDuffie ripped the ball out of Hill's hands. The ball rolled away from Hill and into Edwards' hands. But Edwards had no chance to sprint away from Hill, the league's fastest player.

"I was like, 'Nah, we've got to do something else,'" Edwards said, smiling. "I kind of looked back and I saw my boy B.C., and I trusted him. You've got to have trust to do some stuff like that. I just pitched it back and he did the rest."

Edwards could've given the ball to McDuffie. Or even cornerback Joshua Williams.

"I was over there begging for it, but he ended up hitting B-Cook," Williams said, laughing. "I'm glad because if he throws it to me, I might've gotten tackled."

Edwards made one of the smartest decisions you'll see in the middle of a play: He lateraled the ball to Cook and protected his teammate by blocking tight end Durham Smythe. Cook went untouched by the Dolphins during his thrilling 59-yard return for a touchdown. That's because Cook evaded four Dolphins by reaching a top speed of 21.31 mph, the fastest play by a Chiefs ball carrier this season, according to Next Gen Stats.

"Nah, that's not the fastest," Cook said of his top-end speed. "I ran track in high school, so I tried to bring that out."

Halfway through their season, the Chiefs (7-2) appear to have one of the best defenses in the franchise's 64-year history. General manager Brett Veach and coach Andy Reid agreed to trade Hill to the Dolphins for five draft picks because they wanted to improve the Chiefs defense and better balance the team's roster. Last season, the Chiefs won Super Bowl LVII in part because of an influx of rookie defenders — including McDuffie, Cook, Williams, defensive end George Karlaftis and linebacker Leo Chenal — who were notable contributors. Excluding the offense's giveaway that led to a touchdown in the opening-night loss to the Detroit Lions, the Chiefs have allowed just 15.1 points per game, the second lowest in the league.

"I can probably tell you, halfway through the season, that this is the best defense I've ever played with,"

**RIGHT:** Safety Bryan Cook takes a fumble all the way back for a touchdown to help give Kansas City a 21-0 lead in the win over Miami.

tight end Travis Kelce said. "They come up in huge moments, man. Honestly, they've been saving us in a lot of situations. But that's why you play this team game, man. It's why it's the best game in the world."

The Dolphins entered Deutsche Bank Park with the NFL's top-scoring offense, averaging 33.9 points per game.

Led by their exceptional secondary — including L'Jarius Sneed, safety Justin Reid and McDuffie, Williams, Cook and Edwards — and blitzes from coordinator Steve Spagnuolo, the Chiefs held the Dolphins scoreless in the first half. Just days before kickoff, Hill vowed that he would have an impressive impact for the Dolphins, but he wasn't able to beat the Chiefs with his speed to catch a deep pass.

"We wanted to take that away and make them earn it the hard way," Williams said of Hill, who had eight receptions on 10 targets for 62 yards. "We stayed disciplined."

The Chiefs offense failed to extend the 21-0 lead after halftime. Several mistakes contributed to the unit sputtering. Often, Mahomes didn't have open receivers downfield. That led to him fumbling while being sacked, just as he did last week in the Chiefs' loss to the Denver Broncos. When Mahomes did throw a deep pass the next drive, receiver Marquez Valdes-Scantling dropped the ball.

In the fourth quarter, the Chiefs had a chance to finish the game on offense by keeping the ball away from the Dolphins with a successful four-minute drive. Instead, the Chiefs punted after just three plays as Mahomes didn't have an open receiver on third-and-1, forcing an incompletion that gave the Dolphins another chance to rally.

The fans, most of whom donned a red Chiefs jersey, hat or scarf, unleashed their second-loudest roar after the two-minute warning.

"The Chiefs fans won that one," Reid said. "It was loud, aggressive, whether they were from Germany or Kansas City or the (United Kingdom). It was something. We can feel that as players and coaches. We appreciate it."

The Dolphins were 31 yards from the end zone with 63 seconds left when their offense lined up for a fourth-and-10 play. Although the Dolphins had an opportunity to tie the game with a touchdown, Spagnuolo unleashed a rare Cover 0 blitz. The combination of the crowd noise and the seven defenders Spagnuolo engaged to blitz against six blockers led to the game's only poor snap. Center Connor Williams' snap to Tagovailoa in the shotgun was to the right. Instead of focusing all of his attention on the errant snap, Tagovailoa fumbled the ball while looking at the Chiefs' blitzers.

Tagovailoa recovered the ball but couldn't attempt a pass, ending the game.

"That was a tremendous achievement," Reid said of his defenders. "Steve Spagnuolo did a great job with scheming it, and the players executed very well."

Inside the Chiefs' smaller-than-usual locker room, almost every player mentioned two parts of the game they promised to not forget: the tremendous atmosphere the fans created and the defensive trifecta generated by McDuffie, Edwards and Cook.

The game-winning touchdown was even more remarkable, Williams said, because he and his teammates in the secondary talked earlier in the week about the possibility of taking advantage of a takeaway with a lateral.

"The (coaches) are always telling us to capitalize on defense and score when you get an opportunity," Williams said. "We were saying, 'If somebody gets the ball and you're about to go down, toss to somebody who's open.'

"We were kind of joking, but it played out today exactly how we planned it." ■

LEFT: Wide receiver Skyy Moore and the Chiefs were feeling good after paying off their trek to Germany with a win.

# Rashee Rice

**Chiefs Rookie Breaks Out Thanks to Connection with Patrick Mahomes**

BY NATE TAYLOR ———————— DECEMBER 1, 2023

Their relationship began with a scenario similar to one of America's most popular TV shows, "The Bachelor."

Although Rashee Rice wasn't participating in a dating show, he was one of the few contestants — a small group of talented receivers who were less than a month from being NFL rookies — on the indoor field in Fort Worth, Texas. Rice and a few other receivers, such as Zay Flowers and Quentin Johnston, were given an opportunity in April to make a strong first impression on Kansas City Chiefs quarterback Patrick Mahomes, the league's reigning MVP.

As part of his usual offseason routine, Mahomes held one of his passing sessions on TCU's campus, another day for him to continue strengthening his on-field connection with his pass catchers, teammates such as All-Pro tight end Travis Kelce and receivers Marquez Valdes-Scantling, Skyy Moore and Kadarius Toney. Mahomes enjoys the workouts because he serves as a conductor, a quarterback who wants to see how his pass catchers run a bunch of routes based on scenarios he creates, repetitions against various zone coverages that require everyone to use their imagination because no defenders are on the field.

The session also served as one of the final parts of the Chiefs' pre-draft preparations. Mahomes knew that general manager Brett Veach and coach Andy Reid were intrigued to hear his thoughts on how Rice, Flowers and Johnston performed.

Rice ran every route that day with one goal: making sure Mahomes remembered him.

"I've always had a good quarterback, but I've never really had a quarterback that I was 100 percent confident that he knew exactly what I was thinking during a certain play," Rice said. "It just clicked."

Mahomes' notes to Veach and Reid were concise. Rice was faster than he expected. Mahomes noticed that Rice could slow down his route just a bit, as if settling between two zone defenders, before making the catch and showing acceleration up the field. The biggest takeaway: Rice was a great listener.

"He had a good grasp of (the) feel," Mahomes said of Rice. "If he made a mistake, he would fix it the next time."

Before the Chiefs' practice Thursday, Rice shared that he's never watched an episode of "The Bachelor,"

even though he understands the show's premise. But Rice knew the draft in late April was when he was going to be selected by a team and paired with his next quarterback.

Flowers and Johnston were chosen by other teams, the Baltimore Ravens and the Los Angeles Chargers, respectively, ahead of Rice in the first round. Midway through the second round, Veach turned to his personnel staff, Reid and club owner Clark Hunt.

"Let's just go up and get our guy," Veach said in the Chiefs' draft room with Mahomes on his mind.

Veach's decision — moving the Chiefs up nine spots after executing a trade with the Detroit Lions to acquire the 55th pick — pleased Mahomes. Rice, who watched the draft in his hometown of North Richland Hills, Texas, smiled when he showed his family and friends his smartphone displaying the name of his new quarterback. Mahomes called Rice to congratulate him within minutes of his selection.

After their short chat on the phone, one of Rice's first thoughts was about catching his first passes from Mahomes that fateful day before they became teammates.

"He made me seem like I was running the best routes in the world," Rice said of Mahomes. "(He was) just putting (the ball) exactly where it needed to be."

———

Seven months later, the Chiefs are in the midst of one of their biggest surprises of the season: Rice has become the team's most productive wide receiver.

"Patrick is very much like a coach and a GM when he sees talent," offensive coordinator Matt Nagy said Thursday of Mahomes. "He's able to see these guys and then it's a matter of (discussing) what they do well and how do we help fit that into the offense. He's a great eye for that. It's a credit to Brett Veach, his personnel department and Coach Reid for finding Rashee."

Through 11 games, Rice leads the Chiefs' receivers with 44 receptions on 56 targets for 527 yards and five

**RIGHT:** Rookie receiver Rashee Rice was a revelation for the Chiefs with 79 catches for 938 yards and seven touchdowns during the regular season.

touchdowns. Kelce, a future Hall of Famer, is the lone pass catcher who has generated more production — 70 receptions on 88 targets for 732 yards and five touchdowns — than Rice.

The Chiefs' prime-time game Sunday against the Green Bay Packers, at historic Lambeau Field, will provide a marquee stage — and perhaps the next pivotal moment — in Rice's blossoming career. He is emerging as Mahomes' second go-to option, having led the Chiefs with eight receptions for a career-high 107 yards and a touchdown last week in a comeback victory over the Las Vegas Raiders.

"He's a guy who wants it," Mahomes said of Rice after the game. "That's the biggest thing. He wants to be great. He has a chance to be a great receiver in this league, and we're going to continue to push him to be that.

"He'll just say, 'I'm going to be there. I'm going to do what I need to do to get myself open. I'm going to make something happen with it.' That's the type of guys you want."

During his college career at SMU, Rice was a consistent and durable playmaker who scored 25 touchdowns. As a senior last year, he led all FBS receivers in receiving yards per game (112.9), finishing with 1,355 yards in 12 games.

At age 23, Rice was also one of the most experienced prospects in his draft class, a factor the Chiefs felt would help him get on the field quickly while he continued to learn Reid's complex playbook. The team's scouts believed Rice was versatile enough to play each of the Chiefs' three primary receiver positions.

During the offseason, Veach and Reid made several calculated gambles to bolster the Chiefs' receiver position. They didn't re-sign veteran receiver JuJu Smith-Schuster, who joined the New England Patriots via free agency on a three-year, $25.5 million contract with $16 million guaranteed. The Chiefs didn't sign Odell Beckham Jr. or DeAndre Hopkins, either. Instead, they used most of their salary-cap space to acquire a trio of quality defenders — defensive end Charles Omenihu, linebacker Drue Tranquill and safety Mike Edwards.

Listed at 6-foot-1 and 204 pounds, Rice was the No. 82 player in The Athletic analyst Dane Brugler's ranking of the top 300 draft prospects in 2023. He was also ranked as Brugler's 11th-best receiver, which made Veach's trade with the Lions — exchanging picks No. 63, 122 and 249 for the 55th and 194th picks — a bit of a risky move. The Chiefs made Rice the seventh receiver

selected in the draft, ahead of players such as Marvin Mims Jr., Jalin Hyatt and Josh Downs.

"He was a guy that the contested catch and the run-after-the-catch was something that really stood out," Veach said of Rice then. "It makes sense to find a guy that can do a lot of things that he can do. He's almost like a running back after the catch."

At the time, the Chiefs expected Rice to be a dependable backup, whether late in his rookie year or later in his rookie contract.

Rice, though, planned to exceed the Chiefs' expectations before training camp started.

"I knew that just getting drafted by the Chiefs, I had a great quarterback," Rice said. "They didn't pick me up just to be a part of the team. They wanted me to contribute."

Camp began with Rice, smiling in his new red practice jersey, walking down the large hill on Missouri Western State's campus that led to the practice fields. He shouted three words.

*First day, baby!*

Reid's camps always begin with a soft launch, a trio of truncated practices meant to mostly acclimate the quarterbacks and rookies. With most veterans yet to report, Reid required Rice to participate in every possible repetition — in the offense's install period, seven-on-seven and the team period in the red zone. Another route, another route, another route. Reid wanted Rice to run his routes faster, too.

Ahead of camp, Rice did his best to slim down, trimming 12 pounds. An hour into his first practice, Rice tried to go back into the huddle. But his body stopped him. Reid responded by pausing the practice. Then Rice threw up his breakfast.

"That just means I'm working as hard as I can," Rice said then, "so that I don't puke anymore."

Linebacker Leo Chenal, a second-year player, knew the feeling. He, too, vomited, twice in the end zone, during the team period in the red zone, in his opening camp practice.

"When I heard about that, I'm like, *'Duuuuuude,'*" Chenal said early in camp, laughing. "A lot of people assume he's out of shape. But you've got all those nerves, too, on top of that 100-degree heat and the rookies taking all the snaps."

A week later, with the veterans on the fields, an injury led to Rice receiving lots of reps with the first-team offense. Toney, a three-year veteran, tweaked one of his knees just seconds into the first full-team practice, an injury that damaged the meniscus and forced him to have surgery.

Rice became the receiver who benefited most from Toney's absence. Early in camp, Rice impressed Mahomes and Reid. In a red zone period, Mahomes

<hr>

LEFT: Rashee Rice had a big game in the New Year's Eve win over the Bengals with five catches for 127 yards.

**LEFT:** Rashee Rice celebrates his touchdown in the AFC Wild Card win over the Dolphins. Rice had eight catches for 130 yards and a touchdown in the victory.

threw a perfect pass toward the corner of the end zone, the ball placed just past the outstretched left arm of cornerback Trent McDuffie. Rice made a diving catch, prompting cheers from many of his teammates.

The more Rice did well in camp, the more assignments and routes — intermediate, deep and even double-move routes — Reid and Nagy gave him. On several occasions, Nagy compared Rice's experience early in the season to drinking water from a firehose.

"I was excited to run those routes since I didn't get the opportunity to run them in college," Rice said. "It was also exciting for me to try certain routes on guys like Trent and (cornerback L'Jarius) Sneed, top guys in the league. Executing those plays kind of justified to myself that I'm able to succeed.

Midway through camp, Moore, a second-year receiver, made a prophetic statement about Rice to receivers coach Connor Embree.

"I told you he's the shallow cross king," Moore said.

"He's JuJu," Embree replied.

Smith-Schuster, who worked alongside Kelce last season, produced 78 receptions for 933 yards and three touchdowns, helping the Chiefs become Super Bowl LVII champions.

Similar to Smith-Schuster, Rice has made plenty of highlights that showcase his physicality and strength in the open field. Often catching the ball behind the line of scrimmage or while working underneath against zone coverages, Rice leads the NFL in yards after the catch per reception (8.2) among the 48 receivers with at least 30 targets.

"It's kind of cool being compared to JuJu," Rice said, smiling. "Obviously, they're going to compare me to him earlier in the year than later because they haven't seen me make as many plays yet. Growing up, I was just trying to learn from Julio Jones and DeSean Jackson.

"Anything I could take from all of those guys, I just put it in my game. Maybe I'll look like Julio on one play and JuJu on the other. It doesn't matter as long as I make the play."

Few rookie receivers have generated impressive statistics under Reid during his 25 years as a head coach. In 2009 with the Philadelphia Eagles, Jeremy Maclin had 56 receptions on 91 targets for 773 yards, the second most for a rookie, behind Jackson (912), under Reid. When asked to compare the two receivers, Reid shared this week that he believes Rice is a stronger player than Maclin was as a rookie.

In the Chiefs' win over the Minnesota Vikings in early October, Rice caught a quick pass from Mahomes late in the fourth quarter, a reception made behind the line of scrimmage on a run-pass option. Knowing he needed to stay in bounds, Rice ran through rookie cornerback Mekhi Blackmon for an 8-yard gain that resulted in a first down.

Two weeks later, in the Chiefs' victory over the Los Angeles Chargers, Rice finished a 12-yard gain on a screen pass by trucking safety Dean Marlowe, a level of physicality that led Kelce to praise his teammate after the play by barking over and over again.

"He can fly around with the best of them, man," Kelce said of Rice last week. "Seeing him keep developing into the player that he is, and the weapon he is for the offense, is fun to watch."

Against the Miami Dolphins earlier this month, Rice ran through the tackling attempt of outside linebacker Bradley Chubb to score an 11-yard touchdown.

"To be honest, I'm looking for every moment possible to try to run somebody over," Rice said in October.

Even Mahomes has his own comparison for Rice. In late August, before Rice made his NFL debut, Mahomes said the rookie's combination of strength and speed reminded him of another receiver and former teammate: Sammy Watkins, the 2014 first-round pick who helped the Chiefs win Super Bowl LIV.

Two days later, a reporter shared Mahomes' projection with Rice.

"Pat said that?" Rice said.

When Mahomes' words were confirmed, Rice immediately nodded his head in agreement.

"Yes!" Rice said, laughing and smiling. "If Pat said it, then, yeah."

---

Two of Rice's best traits have contributed to his success. He is inquisitive, leading him to ask more questions to coaches and veteran players than the typical rookie. The second attribute — being an attentive listener — was instilled in him by Gloria Rice, his grandmother who is a retired U.S. Postal Worker and Army veteran who served in the Gulf War.

"She always told me something, and I was young: I wanted to have the last word," Rice said. "As I started growing up, I learned the more you listen, the more you learn."

Since joining the Chiefs, Rice has always been eager to start a conversation — or extend one — while seeking one more tip of information from Reid, Nagy or Embree. Rice's two most prominent mentors in the locker room have been Mahomes and Kelce.

During practices, Rice has received compliments from Kelce after running a route. Kelce has emphasized a four-word phrase multiple times to Rice, a mantra that has led him to have a stellar connection with Mahomes: *Think like the quarterback.*

"Sometimes in college, I just had to run certain

routes even if it was implied that I wouldn't get open, just because I had to run the full offense," Rice said. "But here, you can add a little bit of your own game to it just because Pat is adding his own game.

"I've just always had a good feel for the zones. It just so happens that I get to do it with Pat."

Mahomes is one the league's best passers when performing out of the structure of the designed play, a gunslinger who can create excellent improvisational completions while scrambling out of the pocket. As Reid's playbook has evolved over his 11 years in Kansas City — incorporating the Air Raid, the pistol and old-school option offenses — Kelce has studied each variation of the Chiefs' passing concepts and has found the spaces, often in the short and intermediate areas of the field, where he can ad-lib his route without disrupting those of his teammates.

In Mahomes' sixth season as the Chiefs' leading man, Rice has progressed in the offense faster than any rookie receiver before, doing so by learning when and how to modify his route based on the coverage of the opposing secondary and the offense's formation. Mahomes explained that he was surprised when the Vikings played a certain version of Cover 1 behind a five-man blitz in the red zone. But Mahomes saw Rice adjust his slant and win the one-on-one matchup, beating cornerback Byron Murphy Jr. for an 8-yard touchdown reception.

Two of Rice's touchdowns, against the Lions and Chargers, came when he improvised after his initial route, finding space between defenders in the back of the end zone to get open for Mahomes.

"He's working to be more Patrick-friendly," Reid said. "There's a lot that goes into that. A lot of it is just playing but being willing to fit your game into the offense's game and how Patrick sees things. He's done a nice job of being open that away, listening and deciphering what defenses work with what routes and how to manipulate that."

Rice's breakout performance against the Raiders included such a moment. In the third quarter, he was supposed to run a 5-yard comeback route toward the middle of the field from the slot. But two seconds after the snap, Mahomes escaped the pocket, scrambling to the left. Rice responded by doing an about-face, locating the nearest defender in the Raiders' zone coverage, linebacker Robert Spillane, and getting behind him while running to the sideline. Mahomes started to unleash his pass the moment Rice raised his right arm. The play ended in a 19-yard completion, including 5 yards after the catch.

"The exciting part that we look at it, as a staff, is this is just the beginning with him," Nagy said. "We're seeing growth, we're seeing how to use him. But he can get a lot better, which is great. I think that's what Patrick sees."

Rice's favorite play of the season was his biggest highlight against the Raiders. On a third-and-6 snap early in the fourth quarter, Reid and Nagy trusted Rice with a play designed for him. The Raiders were in zone coverage and Rice ran a shallow crossing route, catching the ball before reaching the line to gain for the first down. But Rice displayed his after-the-catch burst to run away from cornerback Nate Hobbs, gaining 34 yards after the ball reached his hands for an exceptional 39-yard touchdown. Rice also received a well-timed block downfield from Valdes-Scantling.

Mahomes and Kelce were the first to congratulate Rice in the end zone.

"In the draft, some (analysts and coaches) were worried about my speed, saying I was slow," Rice said. "I got a perfect pass from Pat to catch the ball in stride and show the world that I can run."

Finishing with a game-high 107 yards, Rice became the first Chiefs receiver in 21 regular-season games to record more than 100 yards, the last coming when Smith-Schuster (124) and Valdes-Scantling (111) both did it in Week 7 last season.

Rice's next receiving touchdown will tie him for the most by a rookie in the franchise's 64-year history.

Ahead of facing the Packers, Mahomes' message for Rice earlier this week was to not be satisfied with his performance against the Raiders. Rice responded he way he often does: nodding in agreement.

"It felt great to show everybody I can do that, but we have a lot more season left," Rice said. "There should be many more games like that." ∎

# Costly Errors

### Another Mistake by a Receiver Costs Chiefs Another Win

———————— BY NATE TAYLOR

Teammate after teammate tried their best to slow down Patrick Mahomes — his movement toward down judge Mike Carr, the blistering expletives he shouted at the entire officiating crew and his almost unbridled fury — after the Kansas City Chiefs experienced another gut-punch of a loss Sunday.

Once Mahomes, the Chiefs' star quarterback, began exhaling, he was surrounded by tight end Blake Bell, left guard Joe Thuney, rookie left tackle Wanya Morris, right guard Trey Smith and center Creed Humphrey.

With one minute remaining, the scoreboards at Arrowhead Stadium showed the Buffalo Bills leading 20-17 with possession of the ball. Mahomes and everyone else on the Chiefs' sideline, however, felt they should have been leading the Bills by at least three points before an extra-point attempt. Instead, the Chiefs' most impressive offensive play of the season — an across-the-field lateral from tight end Travis Kelce leading to a potential game-winning touchdown — was marred by a penalty, a flag thrown by Carr.

In a cruel twist for everyone who donned red at Arrowhead, the player who committed the offside penalty was the same player who scored the touchdown: receiver Kadarius Toney.

Toney lined up in the neutral zone before the play, a second-and-10 snap from the Bills' 49-yard line during the Chiefs' two-minute drill. If Toney had started the play in the proper spot, he would've benefited from one of the most impressive, instinctual plays of the season by Kelce, who caught an intermediate pass from Mahomes, evaded two defenders for a 25-yard gain and then stunned the Bills by unleashing a perfect lateral pass across to the field. Toney, who was wide open, caught Kelce's pass and was never touched as he sprinted into the end zone for a 24-yard touchdown, a score that would've given the Chiefs the lead with 1:25 left in the game.

"It's obviously tough to swallow, not only for me but just for football in general, to take away greatness like that, for a guy like Travis to make a play like that," Mahomes told reporters after the game. "Who knows if we win? I know, as fans, you want to see the guys on the field decide the game."

Once Toney's penalty nullified the viral highlight, the Chiefs never gained another yard. Each of Mahomes' final three passes fell incomplete.

Toney's mistake was just the latest by a Chiefs receiver this season. The list includes pre-snap penalties, bad adjustments on deep routes and dropped passes. Rather than discuss Toney's error, though, Mahomes and coach Andy Reid spent most of their postgame comments criticizing Carr, referee Carl Cheffers and the rest of the officiating crew.

"Very disappointed that it ended the way it did," Reid said. "I never use any of this as excuses, but normally I get a warning before something like that happens in a big game. A bit embarrassing in the National Football League for that to take place. If it's even close, the head coach gets a warning. It's a bit embarrassing. I've been in the league a long time, and I haven't had one like that."

Reid and Mahomes both said Carr should've warned Toney that he had lined up in the neutral zone before the play began, a courtesy some line judges or down judges give to ensure receivers and cornerbacks are in the correct spot. Mahomes, the league's reigning MVP, stressed multiple times that he thought Carr's decision to penalize Toney without a warning changed the outcome of the game.

"It's the call, man, just in that moment," Mahomes said. "It's not even for me. I just know how much everybody puts into this game. I've played seven years and have never had offensive offsides called. That's elementary school. We talk about it: You point to the (line judge or down judge) and it doesn't get called. If it does, then they warn you.

"There was no warning throughout the entire game. Then you wait until there's a minute left in the game to make a call like that? It's tough, man. (I'm at) a loss for words. Regardless if we win or lose, just for it to end with another game where we're talking about the refs, man, it's just not what we want for the NFL and for football."

Last week, the Chiefs felt they didn't receive fair treatment from a different officiating crew in the final minute of their 27-19 loss to the Green Bay Packers.

That game's penultimate play — when receiver

**RIGHT:** Kansas City's defense didn't make life easy on Josh Allen and Buffalo, but there were too many mistakes on the offensive side of the ball to overcome.

Marquez Valdes-Scantling appeared to be interfered with by rookie cornerback Carrington Valentine but a penalty wasn't called — ended in a controversial incompletion. After the game, Mahomes decided to be diplomatic, choosing to not condemn the officials. He instead explained that he felt he should've thrown his deep pass better, placing the ball farther to the left and away from the defender to increase Valdes-Scantling's chance of making the reception.

"(The officials) are human, man," Mahomes said after Sunday's game. "They make mistakes, but it's every week we're talking about something. All I can do is go out there and give everything I have. I'm proud of the guys because that's what we did. Another great game that just ends like that is just tough.

"Let us play the game, man. And then whatever happens, happens. That's what hurts me. You want it to be about your team and that team and see what happens. Then, I can live with the results."

Late in Sunday's game against the Bills, Mahomes noticed Carr throwing his flag at the start of the pivotal second-down play. Mahomes thought Carr was penalizing one of the Bills' defensive linemen for being offside, a penalty that would've given him a free play to throw the ball downfield, which led to his decision to target Kelce.

Before he raged on the sideline, Mahomes said he approached three officials to get an explanation for Toney's penalty. Mahomes said all three officials declined his request.

"I saw the picture — and (Toney) probably is barely offside," Mahomes said. "But for (Carr) to take the game into his hands over a call like that, that doesn't affect the play at all — at all, didn't affect anything — is just tough, man."

CBS' cameras didn't show Toney, or any of the other Chiefs' pass catchers, pointing to Carr or line judge Thomas Eaton before the second-down snap to get confirmation they lined up in the proper spot. After the game, Cheffers, in a pool report, explained that Carr didn't have to give Toney a warning before the play.

"Ultimately, they are responsible for wherever they line up," Cheffers said of Toney. "Certainly, no warning is required, especially if they are lined up so far offsides where they're actually blocking our view of the ball. So, we would give them some sort of warning if it was anywhere close, but this particular one is beyond a warning."

Within seconds of Cheffers announcing Toney's penalty, eliciting groans from the home crowd, CBS

**RIGHT:** Running back Jerick McKinnon punches in the touchdown in the 20-17 loss to the Bills.

78

analyst Tony Romo shared his simple analysis for why the Chiefs left Arrowhead with an 8-5 record.

"These receivers can't get out of the way of hurting this team," Romo said. "Too many times at the end of the game."

Each of the Chiefs' five losses has involved poor execution by their receivers.

- Toney dropped multiple passes, including one that led to an interception return for a touchdown, in the season-opening loss to the Detroit Lions.
- Skyy Moore dropped a perfect pass from Mahomes on fourth-and-2 in the end zone in the loss to the Denver Broncos. In the same game, Valdes-Scantling also fumbled the ball away.
- Valdes-Scantling dropped a potential game-winning touchdown in the final minutes of the Chiefs' loss to the Philadelphia Eagles.
- Against the Packers, Mahomes and Valdes-Scantling failed to complete a deep pass in the fourth quarter that would've put the Chiefs in scoring range. On the next play, a third-down snap, Mahomes watched his intended target, receiver Richie James, fall down while running his route in the middle of the field.

Mahomes is also clearly frustrated because the team's chances of earning the AFC's top playoff seed — including home-field advantage and a first-round bye — are slipping away. The Chiefs have lost four of their last six games, and their odds of finishing atop the AFC have dropped to just 11.4 percent, according to The Athletic's Austin Mock.

After the game, Toney wasn't available to speak with reporters. Kelce also declined to speak to reporters. Mahomes expressed one more reason for his vitriol toward Carr: He believes Kelce's incredible highlight will soon be forgotten.

"That's a Hall of Fame tight end making a Hall of Fame play that won't be shown because (Carr) threw a flag for an offensive offsides," Mahomes said of Kelce. "It takes away from not only this game in this season but from a legendary career that Travis has had. That hurts me because I know how hard he works for it.

"It's a legendary moment, man. It's something that's not taught. It's something only a couple people in this world would even think about doing. For him to make that play ... in that moment, I hope they still show it whenever he goes into the Hall of Fame." ∎

**RIGHT:** Wide receiver Kadarius Toney stood out for the wrong reasons in the loss, with his offsides flag nullifying what appeared to be a miraculous game-winning touchdown.

# The Final Stretch

**Chiefs Far from Perfect but Good Enough Against Patriots**

——————— BY NATE TAYLOR

These Kansas City Chiefs are imperfect. Through 14 games, they fully know they are imperfect, too. During Sunday's 27-17 victory over the New England Patriots, the Chiefs further learned to accept their imperfections.

"You have to find ways to put games together," Chiefs quarterback Patrick Mahomes said from the podium inside Gillette Stadium.

Inside the Chiefs' locker room, pass rusher Chris Jones used just three words to describe the team's performance.

"It was OK," Jones said. "We suffered two (consecutive) games, and we're not used to that. Whatever we want to achieve, we've got the group in here to achieve it. We've got a lot of good veterans to lead the way and the young guys are eager to get better, eager to listen. We'll be OK. There's no panic in here. It's just a sense of urgency to get better."

Across the locker room was receiver Marquez Valdes-Scantling, who expressed confidence that Sunday's win — which was the first leg of a pivotal four-game stretch to end the regular season — can be the start of the Chiefs progressing toward the best version of themselves.

"This is the same group that we had last year that won a Super Bowl and helped Pat win an MVP," Valdes-Scantling said of the Chiefs' skill-position players. "I think guys kind of forget that because we lost one guy (receiver JuJu Smith-Schuster). We've all got faith that we'll keep figuring this thing out."

By beating the Patriots, the Chiefs averted their first three-game losing streak with Mahomes as their starting quarterback. The victory also kept the Chiefs' slim hopes of earning the AFC's top playoff seed — including home-field advantage and a first-round bye — alive. The Chiefs know the only chance they have of achieving that is to sweep their final four opponents, all of which are being led by a backup quarterback.

Before kickoff, Mahomes used his voice to implore his teammates to be the more energetic team. In their previous three games, the Chiefs never led in the first half.

"We wanted to put the pressure on them," Mahomes said.

Sunday was the first game in NFL history to feature two head coaches, Andy Reid (Chiefs) and Bill Belichick

(Patriots), with at least 250 career regular-season wins. As Reid has done in their past matchups, he unveiled one of his most creative plays of the season with the Chiefs inside the red zone. Everything about the play was unusual, too.

Mahomes didn't line up in his usual shotgun spot. Instead, he was in a three-point stance next to running back Jerick McKinnon. Mahomes guessed the last time he lined up in a three-point stance was when he ran the 40-yard dash at the NFL combine in 2017.

"That (play) was sweet," Mahomes said.

After receiving the direct snap, McKinnon, a former quarterback at Georgia Southern, then did something that wasn't designed in the play: He executed a pop pass to rookie receiver Rashee Rice. Although they never tried it in practice the past three weeks, McKinnon told Rice his idea before they entered the huddle.

Rice juggled the misdirection pass behind the line of scrimmage, but then he secured the catch and ran upfield for an easy 4-yard touchdown.

"Last year, we had a little bit more plays like that in the playbook," McKinnon said. "It's always good to run something like that, something a little different. It was fun."

McKinnon knew Rice's seventh touchdown reception of the season would set a Chiefs rookie record.

"I didn't necessarily come to just break rookie records," Rice said. "There's a lot more on the table for me. I told Jet he's a part of history. It's great. I'm pretty sure that play is going to be taken by a lot of other teams. It's pretty cool to execute a trick play like that."

Mahomes also contributed to the play's design. He suggested to Reid that left guard Joe Thuney snap the ball to McKinnon instead of center Creed Humphrey. Mahomes believed that would help confuse the defensive line.

"They kind of pushed the D-line a little over (to the left), thinking that Creed was the center," Mahomes said of the Patriots. "I'm glad that it worked. That's a hard team to score on in the red zone, so to have a play

**RIGHT:** Running back Clyde Edwards-Helaire elevates for the touchdown catch in the 27-17 win over the Patriots. The catch was one of four for 64 yards on the day for Edwards-Helaire.

like that, that we had worked on for a long time, we executed it at a high level."

Of course, the Chiefs (9-5) didn't have perfect execution Sunday against the Patriots (3-11).

On back-to-back possessions, right guard Trey Smith allowed a drive-ending sack and gave up pressure that led to Mahomes throwing a 50/50 pass in the middle of the field that was intercepted by rookie safety Marte Mapu, who took the ball away from tight end Blake Bell. Less than five minutes before halftime, the Patriots held a three-point lead.

The Chiefs responded with the proper level of concentration. Mahomes led them on four consecutive drives that produced points.

"He's been focused more than I've ever seen him focused," tight end Travis Kelce said of Mahomes. "I don't expect that to change going into the end of the season and into the playoffs."

The Chiefs defense was solid, limiting the Patriots to 3.3 yards on 16 rushing attempts.

Coordinator Steve Spagnuolo called blitzes early and often to have his players swarm quarterback Bailey Zappe, sacking him four times and preventing the Patriots from scoring on their first five drives after halftime. Zappe's first pass in the third quarter was intercepted by linebacker Willie Gay, who retreated to cover tight end Pharaoh Brown before catching the ball near the sideline.

"Willie made a hell of a play," linebacker Nick Bolton said. "We needed that at that time. We've kind of been down at creating turnovers and giving the offense a short field. It's something we've got to keep building on. It's something we're going to try to do more."

Two plays later, running back Clyde Edwards-Helaire produced an even more impressive individual highlight when he improvised in the end zone while Mahomes ad-libbed outside of the pocket, the play resulting in a 6-yard touchdown completion. The 5-foot-7 Edwards-Helaire finished the play by making the Chiefs' best high-point catch of the season, as he elevated over linebacker Jahlani Tavai to make the reception in the back of the end zone.

"I love that dude, man," Kelce said of Edwards-Helaire, who had his best performance of the season, finishing with 101 all-purpose yards on 17 touches. "He's been playing his tail off, waiting for his opportunity. He's the unsung hero for today. That's for damn sure."

Once again, the Chiefs offense made it tough on their defense. Ten of the Patriots' points were the byproduct of giveaways by the Chiefs offense, two in-terceptions that were errors committed by the pass catcher — Bell and receiver Kadarius Toney — not the quarterback. Mahomes, who expressed his frustration at Toney on the sideline, still completed 27 of his 37 attempts for 305 yards and two touchdowns.

Mahomes said Sunday was the first step in the Chiefs' mission to sweep their final four games before the postseason. Mahomes doesn't expect perfection next week when the Chiefs host the Las Vegas Raiders on Christmas Day. He just knows his message for teammates will likely be similar to one he's made several times this season.

"We've just got to continue to make it a full game," Mahomes said. "That's the biggest thing. Just trying to continue to have a full game of excellent football is something we'll continue to strive for." ∎

**LEFT:** Safety Justin Reid makes one of his eight tackles in the win over New England.

Chiefs 25, Bengals 17 | December 31, 2023 | Kansas City, Missouri

# Hail to the Chiefs Defense

Second-Half Shutout Secures AFC West Crown

———————— BY NATE TAYLOR

Steve Spagnuolo went around the Kansas City Chiefs' celebratory locker room Sunday night and kept uplifting his players with his actions.

Spagnuolo, the veteran defensive coordinator, wrapped his arms around Chris Jones, hugging the Chiefs' best pass rusher as tight as he could. A few moments later, Spagnuolo took a knee in front of the defensive backs for a photo. Spagnuolo, with his nose still red from the near-freezing temperature at Arrowhead Stadium, posed by pointing to his players, a group that led the Chiefs to their latest AFC West crown.

In response, several of the Chiefs' defenders — many of them donning a commemorative ballcap or T-shirt — credited Spagnuolo's aggressive coaching style and play calling for generating the biggest highlights in the Chiefs' 25-17 win over the Cincinnati Bengals, a comeback victory that clinched another playoff spot.

The Chiefs (10-6) entered Sunday's game allowing just 17.7 points per game, the second fewest in the league. But the Bengals scored 17 points before halftime, building a 10-point lead by converting short third-down snaps and benefiting from the scrambling ability of backup quarterback Jake Browning.

"We just needed a spark, man," safety Justin Reid said. "Nobody needs to be a Superman or play hero ball. But when it's your chance to make a play, we need somebody to go be that spark to electrify everything because one play makes a difference."

Indeed, the play that started the Chiefs' rally came with seven minutes left in the third quarter, a fourth-and-1 snap for the Bengals at their opponent's 6-yard line.

Spagnuolo countered the Bengals' jumbo formation, including six linemen and two tight ends, with the Chiefs' goal-line personnel, featuring six linemen, two linebackers and two safeties. Anticipating a running play, Spagnuolo called a blitz. Willie Gay Jr., the Chiefs' most athletic linebacker, split center Ted Karras and right guard Alex Cappa to tackle running back Joe Mixon 3 yards behind the line of scrimmage. Watching from the sideline, Spagnuolo celebrated with a fist pump.

"The whole D-line had a good surge on the play, and I just put my invisible suit on and ran through that (lane)," Gay said. "That's a little joke we say in the linebacker room. I was unblocked, and I was thankful to be

there to make the play."

Defensive end Mike Danna said Gay's highlight was like the Chiefs connecting on a power hook in a heavyweight fight, one that knocked the Bengals (8-8) backward. In their final four possessions, the Bengals never came close to having another scoring opportunity.

The Chiefs defense improved its points-per-game average by shutting out the Bengals in the second half, which was essentially required for the unit because the offense, led by quarterback Patrick Mahomes, failed to score a touchdown after its opening possession.

The second half featured the Chiefs playing their best version of Martyball, the old-school strategy of former coach Marty Schottenheimer — including many handoffs to the running back, a highlight or two from the passing attack and the defense dominating the opposing offense to control the tempo. The Chiefs rode that style to seven playoff appearances in eight years in the 1990s.

"This is the way that the Chiefs can still win the Super Bowl," CBS analyst Tony Romo said. "You're not necessarily lighting up the scoreboard, but this defense is (on a) record pace in a lot of categories. It's been since 1995 that they've given up this low amount of yards (and) 2014 since the points per game (were this low). You can rely on them in key moments."

Time after time after time, coach Andy Reid, known for his offensive innovations, trusted his defense — and kicker Harrison Butker, who made a career-high six field goals.

"I let the defense down last week," Mahomes said of the Chiefs' 20-14 loss to the Las Vegas Raiders. "They played their tails off. The two turnovers were 14 points. That changed the entire game, obviously.

"This week, especially after we had the fumble, I tried to do a great job of when it wasn't there deep, get it to underneath guys and try to get the first down. If not, we can punt, man. I know that's not how I've always rolled, but we can punt. The defense can get us the ball back, and we're going to find ways to win games. It's different, man, to have this good of a de-

**RIGHT:** Safety Mike Edwards and the Kansas City defense pitched a shutout in the second half of the 25-17 win over Cincinnati.

fense that shuts the door on some great offensive players. It's going to keep us in every single game."

Chiefs cornerback L'Jarius Sneed delivered a memorable performance.

When Sneed arrived at Arrowhead, he wasn't sure he'd be available to play. In last week's game, Sneed sustained a strained right calf injury that forced him to miss three practices. Sneed said he decided to suit up two hours before kickoff after testing his calf on the field with a few drills.

"God carried me this long," said Sneed, who hasn't missed a game this season. "I just went out there with faith."

Sneed was plenty motivated, too. On Thursday, Ja'Marr Chase, the Bengals' best receiver, said nothing impressed him about the Chiefs' secondary.

"They can take it how they want it; I don't care," Chase said of the Chiefs. "I know what I see on paper. I know what I see in-game. That's why they double everybody because they can't do it one-on-one. ... It's not like they've got a superstar on their defense."

As the Chiefs' shadow cornerback, the defender whose biggest responsibility is covering the opponent's best receiver, Sneed lined up across from Chase on 21 of his 34 routes, surrendering just two receptions for 27 yards, according to Next Gen Stats. Sneed stuck as close as he could to Chase as an intimidation tactic, even after plays, and shoved him a few times.

Chase finished with just three receptions on seven targets for 41 yards. Sneed had three tackles and one pass breakup and, continuing his season-long roll, didn't allow a touchdown in coverage.

"We had some words," Sneed said of Chase. "I went up to him after the game. I told him, 'Good game.' But, you know, check the stats."

Most of the Chiefs' six sacks were the byproduct of their secondary smothering the Bengals' receivers, too. Safety Justin Reid had two sacks and two pass breakups.

The Chiefs secured their eighth consecutive divisional crown, surpassing the Los Angeles Rams (1973-79) for the second-longest streak in league history. Only the New England Patriots (2009-19) have had a longer streak.

For the first time since 2018, when Mahomes became their starting quarterback, the Chiefs earned their division title through the stellar play of their defense.

"Every year is different, and we've had adversity in some of the other years where we've won the West," Chiefs owner Clark Hunt said. "I do think that adversity can be beneficial by the time you get to the play-offs because the playoffs are never going to be easy. It speaks to the character of the team, and that'll benefit us going forward."

The Chiefs know they have one of the league's best defenses, a group that can be compared with the Baltimore Ravens and San Francisco 49ers.

The last player inside the Chiefs' locker room to take off his jersey and shoulder pads was Gay, who spent much of the team's celebration dancing and controlling the hip-hop music that blared through a large portable speaker. When Gay stopped dancing, he was already eager to return to Arrowhead in two weeks when the Chiefs will begin their postseason run, the next phase in their quest to become the league's first repeat champion in two decades.

"We're ready for the playoffs, man," Gay said. "We're ready to roll." ∎

---

**LEFT:** The swarming Kansas City defense limited Cincinnati to just 263 total yards in the win.

# Patrick Mahomes

**Inside the Chiefs QB's Toughest Year**

BY NATE TAYLOR ———————— JANUARY 11, 2024

Patrick Mahomes was tired. His last day of 2023 was a work day, and a trying one at that.

As the quarterback and leader of the Kansas City Chiefs, Mahomes engineered another double-digit comeback in a victory, this time over the Cincinnati Bengals. The win achieved what the Chiefs thought would happen just a few days after Thanksgiving Day: They locked up their eighth consecutive AFC West divisional crown and finally clinched a playoff spot.

That night, though, one of Mahomes' ankles was hurting. One of his shoulders was sore, too. And mentally, he needed a break. The three most prominent members of the Chiefs organization — club owner Clark Hunt, coach Andy Reid and general manager Brett Veach — knew this, even though Mahomes said that night what most veteran quarterbacks say when the regular-season finale is reduced to a meaningless exhibition: the decision will be up to Coach.

Before resting last week, Mahomes experienced the most difficult season of his seven-year career, a 16-game journey that oftentimes left him exasperated.

"You're not always going to win 14, 13 games every single season," Mahomes said. "It's, 'Can you stay with the process every single day and put your team in the best position to succeed?' Then, let's see what happens."

Before this season, however, Mahomes guiding the Chiefs to that many victories in the regular season was the norm.

This season, the Chiefs won 11 games and entered the NFL postseason as the AFC's No. 3 seed, their lowest seed since 2018, when Mahomes became their starter. Next for Mahomes and his teammates is perhaps the hardest path to the Super Bowl that they've encountered. The Chiefs' postseason — and their quest to become the league's first repeat champion in two decades — will begin in the wild-card round with a Saturday prime-time showdown against the Miami Dolphins.

If the Chiefs win the lone home postseason game they're guaranteed, Mahomes could face a new test next week: His first road playoff game.

"Everything you've worked for all season long is on the line," he said. "Everybody is in the same position. But when you put in the time and effort every single day and you spend time away from your family, it's for these moments.

"It excites me to have that pressure on you to go out there and try to perform at the highest level. This is what you watch growing up. You watch these playoff games."

At age 28, Mahomes is many things. He's the greatest player in the Chiefs' 64-history. He's the unquestioned face of the NFL. He's also in the prime of his career — the NFL's reigning MVP, the MVP of Super Bowl LVII and a two-time Super Bowl champion. And because of his past success, Mahomes is the most successful quarterback in this year's tournament, having won 11 playoff games with a quarterback rating, through 14 games, of 107.4, the highest in the Super Bowl era among passers with at least 10 starts.

But another reason why Mahomes was tired after the Chiefs' win over the Bengals is that, for the first time in his career, he was unable to lift the Chiefs offense to the realm of the league's most potent, entertaining units. Even though the Chiefs beat the Bengals by scoring 25 points, the final 19 points were scored by Harrison Butker, the kicker.

Perhaps the weirdest part of the Chiefs season is that Mahomes' yards per game (261.4), yards per attempt (7) and giveaways (17) were all the worst in his career.

The biggest question for Saturday's game — and however far the Chiefs' postseason run goes — is can Mahomes summon enough individual greatness, leadership and composure to propel the offense to be effective enough for the team to win another championship?

"This is when the best football is played," Mahomes said. "All the mistakes are magnified, but all the successes are magnified. You go out with the mentality that I'm going to put my best effort forward and see what happens."

His season was disrupted before his first passing repetition in training camp.

**RIGHT:** The 2023 season was far from smooth sailing for Patrick Mahomes and the Chiefs, but still culminated in a Super Bowl LVIII triumph.

In July, Mahomes arrived at Missouri Western State in St. Joseph, Mo., for the Chiefs' camp eager to strengthen his on-field chemistry with Kadarius Toney, the team's projected No. 1 receiver. Toney joined the Chiefs via a trade with the New York Giants midway through last season. Known for his dynamic, elusive abilities, Toney played a pivotal role in the Chiefs' comeback win over the Philadelphia Eagles in Super Bowl LVII, scoring a touchdown and producing the longest punt return in Super Bowl history. Veach and Reid chose to not sign a veteran receiver — such as Odell Beckham Jr., DeAndre Hopkins or Adam Thielen — in the offseason because they believed Toney, with a full offseason and camp to fully grasp Reid's complex playbook, could have a breakout season, a player capable of becoming the team's next star receiver.

Minutes into the opening practice of camp, Toney damaged the meniscus in his knee when he tried to change directions after catching the punt, an injury that required surgery and forced him to miss camp and the preseason.

Mahomes' season was also disrupted before his first passing attempt in the Chiefs' season opener.

Two days before hosting the Detroit Lions, Mahomes and the rest of the offense were going through reps in the red zone when tight end Travis Kelce hyperextended his right knee. The injury forced Kelce to miss the game, which the Chiefs lost 21-20. The game's outcome was determined by a decision Reid later regretted: Toney, who just returned from his injury, played 16 snaps (25 percent). Mahomes targeted Toney five times, which tied for the team high. But Toney's performance was disastrous. He dropped four catchable passes, including one on which the ball went through his hands and directly to Lions rookie safety Brian Branch, who returned the interception 50 yards for a touchdown

Late in the fourth quarter, with the Chiefs trailing by one point, Reid and offensive coordinator Matt Nagy had the perfect play called against the Lions' zone coverage. Running a deep over route, Toney was wide open for what would've been at least a 25-yard completion, a connection that likely would've put the Chiefs in position for a game-winning field goal. Mahomes threw his pass a few inches behind Toney, thinking the receiver was going to slow down to stay between multiple defenders. Toney, in the middle of his route, took his eyes off the ball to locate defenders, which led to his most egregious drop.

Mahomes' reaction after the play would later become symbolic, one that he repeated often throughout this season: His hands on his helmet, his mouth agape in disbelief.

The following Monday, when the Chiefs returned to their training facility, Toney apologized to his teammates, in particular Reid and Mahomes.

"There's no excuse," Toney said then. "There's nothing you can blame it on."

Despite the Chiefs having the league's most talented quarterback, their skill-position players led the league with 38 drops.

"Guys that I've seen catch before didn't necessarily make the catch," Reid said in November.

The Chiefs' wide receivers — Toney, Marquez Valdes-Scantling, Justin Watson, Skyy Moore, Richie James and rookie Rashee Rice — have dropped 25 catchable passes, the most by any receiver group since the 2012 Jacksonville Jaguars.

"Obviously, it's frustrating," said Valdes-Scantling, a six-year veteran. "You want the ball. We know what our standard is, and we're just trying to figure out how to get back to that. It's frustrating that we're not scoring as many points as we have in the past."

In late October, in a road game against the Denver Broncos that featured cold weather, Mahomes played through flu-like symptoms. Mahomes' skill-position teammates didn't help him much. The Chiefs committed a season-high five turnovers in a loss.

"I was (sick), too," backup quarterback Blaine Gabbert said. "I was probably the one that gave it to him."

Five of the Chiefs' six losses included at least one pivotal play during which a receiver dropped an accurate pass from Mahomes — or made a different unforced error.

Most of those moments were followed by Mahomes placing his hands on his helmet with his mouth agape in disbelief.

Another troubling trend is that the lack of production from the receivers has affected Kelce's effectiveness. Midway through the season, opposing defenses used a tactic that the Dolphins first found success with: using two defenders to cover Kelce. Kelce, 34, has scored just one touchdown in the past nine games.

The Chiefs finished the regular season scoring just 21.8 points per game, the third fewest among the league's 14 playoff teams. Mahomes still produced 4,183 yards and 27 touchdowns and, oddly, finished the regular season with the best completion percentage (67.2) of his career. He knows his percentage should be higher, too.

Week after week, Mahomes has expressed confidence in his receivers, even as his frustration began to intensify.

---

**LEFT:** The Chiefs finished the regular season scoring just 21.8 points per game, but Patrick Mahomes still produced 4,183 yards and 27 touchdowns.

"I know how hard these guys work," Mahomes said. A few weeks later, he reiterated his stance: "I believe in these guys."

---

Projecting each NFL playoff team's odds to win the Super Bowl, with wild-card matchup analysis

Performing while displaying his passionate emotions is what Mahomes has also done — the fist-pumping, screaming and flexing celebrations have been captured aplenty.

In the second half of this season, Mahomes' emotions often included new expressions: anger, irritation and agitation.

In the loss to the Bills, when Mahomes realized the player who committed the offside penalty was the same player who scored the touchdown — Toney — he unleashed his most venomous criticism at down judge Mike Carr, the official who threw the flag. A screaming Mahomes had to be restrained by tight end Blake Bell, left guard Joe Thuney, rookie left tackle Wanya Morris, right guard Trey Smith and center Creed Humphrey.

"I just don't like losing," Mahomes said. "Anybody can be frustrated when they lose. It's just about how you respond."

The Chiefs' next game, a win over the New England Patriots, exasperated Mahomes because of how the game ended. In the fourth quarter, the Chiefs had a commanding 17-point lead and possessed the ball. Mahomes told his teammates in the huddle to protect the ball. The drive's first play ended in an interception that wasn't Mahomes' fault.

Mahomes threw a short pass to Toney, who was open in the middle of the field between two defenders. But the ball bounced off Toney's hands and into those of linebacker Jahlani Tavai. Mahomes stormed off the field and to the Chiefs' sideline. When he sat down on the bench, he screamed loud enough for all of his teammates to hear him.

*"I just f—— said it, man!" Mahomes said. "God— it!"*

This season, many analysts have wondered if the Chiefs' struggles on offense are partly due to losing former offensive coordinator Eric Bieniemy to the Washington Commanders. In Mahomes' five previous seasons as a starter, he had the same coordinator: Bieniemy, the former NFL running back. Among his strengths, Bieniemy was known for his ability to hold players accountable to their teammates for on-field decisions and fundamentals. If players made simple

**RIGHT:** The winning recipe for the Chiefs was different in 2023 with more reliance on their defense, but Patrick Mahomes still made the big plays when needed.

mistakes, Bieniemy wasn't shy about informing them with other players and coaches nearby.

More than ever this season, Mahomes has used his voice similar to Bieniemy's style, many players shared.

On Christmas Day, Mahomes loudly challenged his offensive linemen on the sideline to perform better early in the second quarter against the Las Vegas Raiders.

"He's a great leader, he's a relentless guy and he loves to give everything he has for his team," right tackle Jawaan Taylor said of Mahomes. "He's a great guy to play with. His preparation is crazy. If guys need that extra push, he brings that. We definitely feed off of that. When he needs to say something, he will. That's part of being a leader. We're all grown men. We can take (his) leadership."

The biggest reason the Chiefs fell to the Raiders was Mahomes committed two turnovers that resulted in touchdowns on back-to-back snaps. Of course, the Chiefs offense also had two dropped passes, the unit committed six penalties (each drive with a penalty ended without points being scored) and the two giveaways dropped the team into a tie for last in the league in turnover differential (-10), with the Washington Commanders.

In a season-high 58 dropbacks, Mahomes finished with just 235 passing yards, 53 rushing yards and one touchdown. Pro Football Focus' grade of Mahomes' performance was 34.2, the lowest of his career.

LEFT: Patrick Mahomes had to remain patient with a young group of receivers prone to mistakes early in the season. ABOVE: Patrick Mahomes packed the media room as always during Super Bowl LVIII opening night.

"If I'm going to challenge them to be better, I have to be better within the pocket," Mahomes said of his linemen. "I have to trust those guys as much as I talk. A lot of guys are frustrated that we're losing. At the same time, you have to have the right message. The guys know that I believe in them."

Gabbert, a 12-year veteran, has watched Mahomes try to perform well during moments of rage, something Tom Brady often excelled at.

"If you can harness the emotion and channel it positively, that's the best thing," Gabbert said of Brady, his former teammate. "Tom always said, 'I have no friends on the opposing team,' and it held true. He genuinely didn't like the opposing team. That's how he played. That worked for him. Every person is different."

The Chiefs know Mahomes performs his best when he is thriving in his joyful playing style, one filled with creativity and improvisation. The players understand that the best way to help Mahomes get into a rhythm is by being disciplined and limiting their mistakes.

"It's been a cool experience," James said of playing alongside Mahomes for the first time in his six-year career. "He's a great leader, but he's very demanding. He knows what to do, he's telling you what to do and everyone follows his lead. That's greatness, to me."

***

One word Reid, Nagy and quarterbacks coach David Girardi have asked Mahomes to embrace is "adapt."

More than ever before in his postseason career, Mahomes will attempt to be less of a gunslinger. Instead, he will likely try to perfect what most quarterbacks are asked to do when they are labeled "a game manager" instead of "a superstar": ensure the offense plays complementary football.

"He just wants to win," Nagy said of Mahomes. "He's smart enough to understand that every year is different."

This year is different because Mahomes might not be required to be a superhero in the second half of an elimination game, which was required when he orchestrated thrilling comebacks in Chiefs' two Super Bowl victories.

The best part of the Chiefs roster this season is their defense, a unit led by coordinator Steve Spagnuolo, pass rusher Chris Jones and cornerbacks L'Jarius Sneed and Trent McDuffie. The Chiefs will enter Saturday's game against the Dolphins allowing just 17.3 points per game, the second fewest in the league. The Chiefs have yet to surrender 30 points in a game.

With an exceptional defense and kicker, Mahomes has realized his performance against the Bengals — while not as flashy as he would like — can be a proper prescription for success to help the Chiefs reach another Super Bowl. The Chiefs' efficiency, when opportunities arise in the red zone or on deep passes, Mahomes said, will be paramount.

In the win over the Bengals, the Chiefs didn't turn the ball over in the red zone and Mahomes completed two deep passes, with the ball traveling at least 20 yards in the air, for 108 yards, his first game with more than 100 yards on deep passes since Dolphins star receiver Tyreek Hill was with the Chiefs, according to Next Gen Stats.

"That'll help open Travis up because there's so much attention on him in the middle of the field," Mahomes said of Kelce. "If we can show that we can go over the top and hit these deep passes, it'll open him up."

Mahomes hopes his play this postseason is another sign of his maturity as a quarterback and leader, even if his path to the playoffs this season was tougher than usual — and the path ahead, toward another championship, could be the hardest he's ever experienced.

"I'm extremely confident, not only in our offense but in the team," he said. "You see how the defense is playing. Offensively, I feel like we're going to play our best football at the right time. We don't have to score too many points. If we can just score enough points, our defense will shut the door." ∎

**RIGHT:** Ever the leader, Patrick Mahomes hypes the team up with a speech prior to the AFC Championship game road win over the Ravens.

# Cold-Blooded

Chiefs Shrug Off Sub-Zero Conditions to Knock Out Dolphins

——————— BY NATE TAYLOR

In one corner of the Kansas City Chiefs' locker room was L'Jarius Sneed, the team's most experienced cornerback. Sneed, a four-year veteran, is known more for his trash-talking skills on the field than after a game. Late Saturday night, though, Sneed and the rest of the Chiefs, every member having just finished playing in one of the most unusual games of their career, wanted to make a loud statement about their opponent in the wild-card round of NFL playoffs.

"We knew it was going to be a cold game and we knew they weren't used to it," Sneed said of the Miami Dolphins. "We came out and punched them in the mouth. We saw blood."

In the opposite corner of the Chiefs' locker room was left tackle Donovan Smith, a member of the offensive line, a group that spent much of the game stonewalling the Dolphins' pass rushers. As the game progressed, and the Chiefs continued to build their lead, Smith made what he felt was an astute observation of the Dolphins.

"Obviously, you could feel and see that they felt it over there," he said, smiling. "That's why you play the game. You break their will."

For the Chiefs, Saturday's game, a dominant 26-7 victory, proved two things: They are better than the Dolphins — and they are better performers in freezing weather.

At kickoff, the temperature at Arrowhead Stadium was minus-4, making the elimination game the fourth-coldest game in the NFL's 104-year history. The windchill factor, according to NBC, was minus-27. In the middle of the Chiefs' locker room was quarterback Patrick Mahomes, who made just one change to his usual game-day attire under his jersey and helmet: He wore an older red thermal ski mask, the same one he used in previous playoff games.

"It was cold, but you've got to be mentally tough enough to just say, 'It's not going to affect how we play; it's not going to affect my effort,'" said Mahomes, who is 21-6 in his career in games played in 40 degrees or colder, including 10-1 in the postseason. "It wasn't going to be like we were just going to run the ball. We ran the ball well, but at the same time, you have to throw the ball in order to have success in this league. I take that as a challenge."

Because the Chiefs won their eighth consecutive AFC West title, earning the No. 3 seed, and the Dolphins failed to win the AFC East, falling from the No. 2 seed to No. 6, Saturday's much-anticipated rematch was be played at Arrowhead. Of course, the Chiefs felt they were more prepared than the Dolphins for the conditions. The Chiefs practiced outside — in freezing conditions, albeit not minus-4 degrees — Wednesday and Thursday. The Dolphins couldn't do the same while preparing in Miami.

The prime-time showdown was receiver Tyreek Hill's first game at Arrowhead since he was traded in March 2022. He entered the venue wearing just a sweater and sweatpants.

"I'm freezing my balls off out here," Hill said. "S—!"

The Dolphins never led and the Chiefs scored their first touchdown, an 11-yard connection from Mahomes to rookie receiver Rashee Rice, less than five minutes after kickoff.

The Chiefs started the game with three consecutive passes, too.

"We knew that our opponent didn't want to be out here in this cold as much as we did," Rice said. "We took it to the chin and showed our love for the game."

Saturday's game was carried on Peacock, marking the first playoff game in league history to be televised exclusively on a streaming platform. Just before the end of the first quarter, Peacock cameras captured an image that perfectly illustrated just the frigid conditions: icicles on coach Andy Reid's thick, walrus-like mustache.

"The worst thing that could happen is it falls off," Reid said, grinning, his mustache still intact.

Mahomes, throughout his seven-year career, has built an unassailable reputation for playing his best in January and February. Since he became the Chiefs' starter in 2018, each January has started the same way: a playoff run beginning at Arrowhead.

Saturday's game, though, featured a few new details — the coldest game of his career, his quarterback-specific VICIS helmet cracking on a hit from a

**RIGHT:** Patrick Mahomes gets pumped up before the Chiefs' wild-card round game against the Miami Dolphins. Playing in subzero temperatures, Mahomes passed for 262 yards and a touchdown in the win.

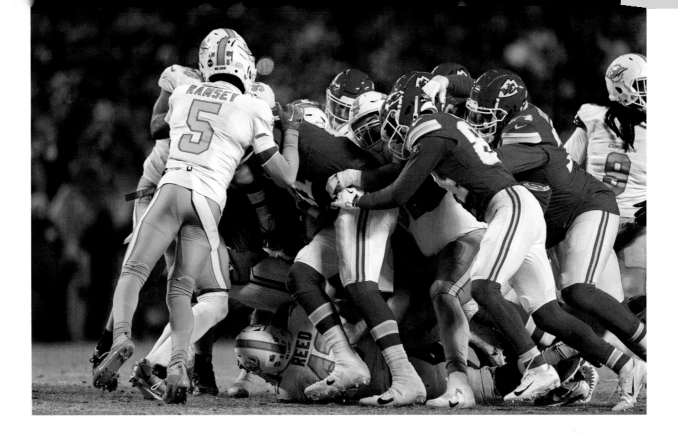

defender and a rookie who produced a breakout performance in his postseason debut. But Mahomes was Mahomes, producing another stellar performance, especially when the Dolphins blitzed. Mahomes' accuracy, even in windy conditions, was excellent. He chose the correct times to scramble and finished with only one negative play, an intentional-grounding penalty.

Perhaps the game's most memorable play was Mahomes' 13-yard scramble in the third quarter, the play featuring helmet-to-helmet contact with Dolphins safety DeShon Elliott. When Mahomes stood up, several teammates pointed out something they had never seen before: a hole in the front, left side of his helmet.

"I was trying to get in that end zone," Mahomes said. "A young Pat would've got in. I'm getting a little old. I try not to do it too much, but it's playoff time. Sometimes you've got to put it on the line.

"I'm sure it had to do with it being really cold. I didn't know it happened in the moment, but I got in the huddle and everybody was telling me. I was, 'I'm not coming out of the game.' It was a first for me."

Mahomes played the next two snaps with the hole in his helmet. Once officials noticed it, they made him get his backup helmet from the bench. Switching helmets didn't feel great, Mahomes said.

LEFT: L'Jarius Sneed breaks up a pass intended for Miami's Tyreek Hill in the second half. The Chiefs limited Hill to eight targets for 52 yards. ABOVE: Despite playing in frigid conditions, the Chiefs offense converted on the ground, rushing for 147 yards on 34 carries.

"We have to talk about where we store the backup (helmet) because it was frozen," he said, smiling.

In the teams' first matchup in Frankfurt, Germany, in early November, the Dolphins blitzed 10 times. But before halftime Saturday night, the Dolphins blitzed Mahomes on 51.9 percent of his 26 dropbacks, according to Next Gen Stats. Without their top three edge rushers (Bradley Chubb, Jaelan Phillips and Andrew Van Ginkel), the Dolphins finished with 18 snaps in which they used Cover 0, a blitz where every offensive skill-position player is guarded by just one defender in man-to-man coverage.

Mahomes was never sacked and the Dolphins' secondary wasn't effective in coverage against Rice and tight end Travis Kelce, who finished with 71 receiving yards on seven receptions.

"We knew they might blitz a little bit, so I tried to have answers for every single play," said Mahomes, who finished with 262 passing yards. "For the most part, I thought I did. Even if I didn't hit it, I was going to the right spot and on time to try to give our guys chances to make plays."

When the Dolphins blitzed — their 18 snaps in Cover 0 were the second most in a game since 2018 — or played zone coverage, Mahomes completed most of his passes when targeting Rice, who finished with 130 yards, the best performance any Chiefs rookie receiver has had in his playoff debut. Rice surpassed the 104 yards that Elmo Wright had in 1971 in an overtime game on Christmas Day against the Dolphins.

"A lot of our offense goes off of whether it's man and zone at the beginning of the play and you'll be able to change your route," Rice said.

As for his record-setting performance, Rice said: "I'm going out there to just get a win, and I look forward to keep putting my name down as much as I can in this program."

For the second time this season, the Chiefs defense, led by coordinator Steve Spagnuolo, swarmed the Dolphins — both quarterback Tua Tagovailoa in the pocket and the skill-position players on the perimeter. Pass rushers George Karlaftis, Chris Jones and Charles Omenihu generated consistent pressure on Tagovailoa, who was sacked twice and threw an interception.

Omenihu was the one who pressured Tagovailoa when he threw his interception, a play that featured one of Spagnuolo's best-disguised coverages. Safeties Mike Edwards and rookie Chamarri Conner showed two-high coverage before rotating to a single-high look, with Conner as the deepest defender, before the snap. But after the snap, Edwards and Conner continue to rotate, switching back to two-high coverage.

"We tried to change some stuff up, and that play kind of throws the quarterback off a lot," Edwards said.

As for his interception, Edwards said: "I didn't catch it like I wanted it to, but I came down with it. That's all that matters."

Even after Hill scored a touchdown on a deep pass, the Chiefs' secondary, led by Sneed and fellow cornerback Trent McDuffie, was exceptional at covering and tackling the Dolphins' receivers. The first time the Dolphins converted on a third-down snap came early in the fourth quarter. Sneed and McDuffie each finished with two pass breakups.

In November, Hill recorded eight receptions on 10 targets for 62 yards. Once again, the Chiefs limited Hill, who had five receptions on eight targets for 62 yards, most of it coming on a 53-yard touchdown pass in the second quarter.

As the Chiefs' shadow cornerback, the defender whose biggest responsibility is covering the opponent's best receiver, Sneed allowed only one reception on eight combined targets to Hill and receiver Jaylen Waddle in the two games. Sneed's favorite moment Saturday game came late in the second quarter, a third-down snap in which he was assigned to guard Hill in press-man coverage. Sneed shoved Hill with both of his hands when the play began. Hill stumbled and fell down, never running his route. Sneed's perfect jam at the line of scrimmage happened in front of the Chiefs' sideline, too, a level of tenacity and ruthlessness that energized his teammates.

"I know what his weakness is and I know what he doesn't like," Sneed said of Hill. "He doesn't like it when people put hands on him. That's what I did." ∎

**RIGHT:** Clyde Edwards-Helaire rushed for 21 yards on seven carries, including a 12-yard run to set up a field goal in the second quarter.

# 'We Earned Everything'

## Chiefs Revel in Road Victory in Front of Raucous Bills Fans

———————— BY NATE TAYLOR

They sprinted to each other, the noise surrounding them beginning to dissipate.

Several yards from one another, linebacker Nick Bolton and quarterback Patrick Mahomes screamed and unleashed their tense emotions with the same celebration: leaping off the artificial turf and pumping their right fist. Several members of the Kansas City Chiefs — players, coaches and athletic trainers — hugged one another, either on the playing surface or the sideline Sunday night. The much-anticipated playoff showdown, the Chiefs' rematch against the Buffalo Bills, this time in the AFC divisional round, wasn't even over yet.

Running back Clyde Edwards-Helaire, though, was the first player to execute the gesture every Chiefs player wanted to do since the team arrived at Highmark Stadium. He stood on a metal bench and waved goodbye to the 70,808 fans, most of them lusting to see the Bills end the Chiefs' quest to become the NFL's first repeat champion in two decades.

"It feels so good when everybody's so loud, and you know it's because they want that other team to succeed," Edwards-Helaire said, smiling. "You can shut all them m—– f—– up, and it's just us on the sideline making noise."

The moment the Chiefs began celebrating — and voicing their vindication at the home crowd — came late in the fourth quarter when the Bills failed to tie the game, missing a field goal attempt that led to the game's final score: Chiefs 27, Bills 24.

For the sixth consecutive season, the Chiefs earned a spot in the AFC Championship Game. Their thrilling victory, one over one of their biggest rivals, guaranteed them another road playoff game next week, a marquee matchup against the Baltimore Ravens, with the winner representing the AFC in Super Bowl LVIII.

"This was so fun," safety Justin Reid said of the Chiefs ending the Bills' season for the third time in the past four years. "The environment was crazy. We don't appreciate all the snowballs (thrown at us), but it still added to it.

"This is one of my favorite games, man. We earned everything. Nothing was easy, and that's a good-ass team. We found a way to come out on top."

Throughout their preparation for Sunday's game, the Chiefs told themselves to embrace a setting they knew would be foreign to most of them: a road playoff game. Since Mahomes became their starting quarterback in 2018, the Chiefs had played in a league-leading 15 postseason games, all of them either at their home venue, Arrowhead Stadium, or a neutral site for that year's Super Bowl.

"I was very excited," Mahomes said. "I knew the fans were going to be rowdy. I think guys took it as a challenge. I love being at Arrowhead and playing in front of that crowd. But when you're on the road, it's you versus them. It's you versus everybody in the stadium. You have to come together as a team."

Inside Highmark's cramped visitors locker room, receiver Marquez Valdes-Scantling smiled when he explained just how unwelcome the Chiefs were in Buffalo, starting Saturday afternoon when they arrived at their hotel.

"It was lit, man," Valdes-Scantling said. "We're pulling up, and everybody is throwing snowballs at the bus and shooting the bird. As soon as we got to the hotel, fans (were) screaming at us. It was a crazy atmosphere. It's a really good feeling to make them all be quiet."

For much of Sunday evening, however, the Bills' fans were raucous, a crowd that threw snow into the sky when quarterback Josh Allen scored the game's first touchdown on a 5-yard run. The Bills scored 10 points in their first two possessions, controlling the game's tempo with their running attack of Allen and running backs James Cook and Ty Johnson. Even after the Chiefs took their first lead late in the second quarter, the Bills responded with a perfect 75-yard drive that ended with Allen running right through the middle of the Chiefs defense for a 2-yard touchdown.

By halftime, the Bills had run 41 plays. The Chiefs, meanwhile, had just 21.

To start the second half, the Chiefs defense — a unit that finished the regular season allowing just 17.3 points per game — was without its top run-stuffing defensive tackle (Derrick Nnadi, who missed the game with an

**RIGHT:** Travis Kelce's welcome to New York was an unpleasant one for Bills fans, as the Chiefs tight end was untouchable, recording five catches on six targets.

> *"I don't think a lot of people gave us a chance. People have counted our offense out all year long. In the biggest game of the year, we showed why we're the defending champs. This was a team win. The offense carried the load."*

elbow injury), its most athletic linebacker (Willie Gay, who aggravated a neck injury) and its top deep safety (Mike Edwards, who sustained a concussion).

"Our depth was tested a lot," linebacker Drue Tranquill said. "I don't think a lot of people gave us a chance. People have counted our offense out all year long. In the biggest game of the year, we showed why we're the defending champs. This was a team win. The offense carried the load."

Because of the deafening crowd noise, Mahomes wasn't sure he communicated his pre-snap adjustment loud enough for Valdes-Scantling to hear before the Chiefs' first play of the third quarter. When the ball was snapped, however, both players recognized the Bills' man-to-man coverage, leading Mahomes to complete a 30-yard pass to Valdes-Scantling, the type of highlight the two struggled to connect on throughout much of the season.

In fact, Mahomes completed all three of his deep passes for 84 yards, his most completions in a game this season, according to Next Gen Stats.

"You have guys like Marquez, who has struggled at points this year, and he made some massive catches for us to help our team win," Tranquill said.

The Chiefs scored a touchdown on their first two possessions of the second half. Mahomes was exceptional, too. He scrambled when necessary, was accurate in windy conditions and threw two touchdowns to tight end Travis Kelce. The second moved the duo ahead of Tom Brady and Rob Gronkowski for the most postseason touchdown connections (16) in NFL history.

When the third quarter ended, Mahomes had completed 14 of his 18 passes for 199 yards without being sacked. But the Chiefs defense had allowed 168 rushing yards, a season high.

**RIGHT:** Bills quarterback Josh Allen fumbles under pressure by the Chiefs defense in the third quarter.

"I went over to the defense and I told them, 'Y'all shut it down and we'll win,'" Mahomes said. "They did. It was a team win. That's what you need in the playoffs."

Emblematic of their season, the Chiefs' offensive players needed to rely on their defensive teammates, too.

Midway through the fourth quarter, the Chiefs had two opportunities to score. Their best opportunity came after the Bills failed to convert on a fake punt deep in their territory. Two plays later, though, Chiefs receiver Mecole Hardman caught a pop-pass behind the line of scrimmage and fumbled when he tried to extend his arms near the pylon, the ball rolling into the end zone and out of bounds for the game's lone turnover.

Hardman touched the ball twice in the game, fumbling each time in the red zone. The second one cost the Chiefs a likely 10-point lead with 11 minutes left.

The Chiefs' next possession didn't last long, either. For the first time, Mahomes had three consecutive failed passing plays, two incompletions and a scramble, near midfield.

"When things went bad, we didn't pin it on each other," pass rusher Chris Jones said. "We all understand that there's more plays to be made. This is one heck of a brotherhood."

The Chiefs shut out the Bills in the fourth quarter.

"That's the epitome of this game, man," Valdes-Scantling said of the Chiefs' teamwork. "The defense played a really good offense, and when they needed to get those stops, they did it. That's who they've been all year. They're so talented at every level, even with the injuries. We don't win without them."

Chiefs defensive coordinator Steve Spagnuolo relied on his best personnel, his dime package. With three safeties on the field — Reid, Deon Bush and rookie Chamarri Conner — the Chiefs' secondary prevented Allen from completing any pass on which the ball traveled more than 15 yards past the line of scrimmage.

Jones was exceptional, too. He created enough pressure to affect Allen's final two pass attempts, both of which fell incomplete.

"It's all about being relentless," Jones said of pursuing Allen. "You're just trying to limit his playmaking ability, especially on the ground. When they go in (shotgun), you don't know if they're going to run it or if it's a pass. You have to transition to pass rushing but also be cognizant of your rushing lanes. All of that's going on in a matter of 2.3 seconds. It takes a lot of

**RIGHT:** Travis Kelce caught two touchdown passes from Patrick Mahomes against the Bills, moving the duo ahead of Tom Brady and Rob Gronkowski for the most postseason touchdown connections in NFL history.

commitment and unselfish play amongst the D-line."

The Chiefs' stop just outside the red zone in the closing minutes forced the Bills to try a potential game-tying field goal.

Bills kicker Tyler Bass entered the game having made all nine of his field-goal attempts in the last two minutes of the fourth quarter when his team was either tied or trailing by three points. But he had never attempted such a kick in an elimination game. Bass watched his 44-yard attempt miss wide right.

Next to Bass was Reid, who waved his arms in the air to signal the kick was no good before the officials near the goal post could signal the same to the fans. Linebacker Leo Chenal showed his astonishment by putting both of his hands on his helmet.

"I just couldn't really see it," center Creed Humphrey, who was sitting on the bench, said of the kick. "I just heard the crowd go silent."

Tranquill, a five-year veteran, said he realized he was going to play in the first championship game of his career when Bills fans began throwing snowballs at him in anger.

"It was unreal," Tranquill said. "There were a lot of words being shouted at their fans. That's why football is awesome. You hear all the talk this week of, 'We finally get them at home!'

"It was a 15-round, blow-for-blow match. I felt (late) in the fourth quarter, in the 15th round, that we had the blows to give to help us win. Man, it's why you train and play this game, for moments like this." ∎

**LEFT:** Coach Andy Reid, quarterback Patrick Mahomes, tight end Travis Kelce, and owner Clark Hunt celebrate in the locker room following the Chiefs' win in Buffalo.

# 'Spags is a Wizard'

## How Steve Spagnuolo Turned Chiefs Defense into One of NFL's Best

BY NATE TAYLOR ——————— JANUARY 26, 2024

Steve Spagnuolo had 10 minutes.

In the first half of last week's AFC divisional playoff game, the Buffalo Bills offense controlled the tempo, scoring 17 points and keeping the Kansas City Chiefs defense on the field for 41 plays. Kansas City failed to limit Buffalo quarterback Josh Allen's scrambling ability, recording only one quarterback hit and allowing the Bills to gain first down after first down.

Standing next to a whiteboard, Spagnuolo, the Chiefs defensive coordinator, started his halftime address with a simple question.

*You guys ready?*

Spagnuolo changed the rushing lanes for the defensive linemen, a move designed to keep Allen in the pocket. He had the secondary play more zone coverage than usual to keep its collective eye on the quarterback and his pass catchers. Spagnuolo used his linebackers in simulated pressures and called more run blitzes on first down.

"We made some (pre-snap) checks that we never practiced," safety Justin Reid said. "We put them in at halftime and went out and executed them on the field. It made all the difference."

"We fixed the things that needed to be fixed," linebacker Drue Tranquill said.

In a major twist, the defense has been the most productive part of a Chiefs team that finds itself back in the AFC Championship Game for a sixth consecutive season. No opponent has scored 30 points on Spagnuolo's unit, which allowed the fewest second-half points (126) in the league. The Chiefs finished the regular season allowing just 17.3 points per game, second-fewest in the NFL.

Allen, one of the league's most talented quarterbacks, had just two games this season in which he averaged 5.5 yards per pass attempt or fewer. Both came against the Chiefs. In Sunday's elimination game, Allen and the Bills didn't score in the fourth quarter of Kansas City's 27-24 victory.

"He's a headache," Spagnuolo said of Allen after the game, his voice filled with relief.

The reason the Chiefs defense could make so many alterations at halftime, Spagnuolo said, was because his players can help solve schematic problems alongside him.

"They love playing together," Spagnuolo said. "I love the chemistry, and it shows on the field. When you get into games like this, chemistry, cohesiveness and guys having confidence in being really bold, is really, really important.

"It's just been beautiful watching these guys jell together."

———

Spagnuolo, whose NFL coaching career began with the Philadelphia Eagles in 1999 and included three years as head coach of the St. Louis Rams, has a longstanding reputation.

He wants to break down the opposing offense's pass-protection rules, then exploit those rules. He wants to call unorthodox plays, too, gambles he hopes are as shocking as they are effective.

"Spags is a wizard, man," defensive end Mike Danna said. "He's got tons of blitzes, and he knows how to get after a quarterback."

Led by defensive tackle Chris Jones and defensive end George Karlaftis (10 1/2 sacks each), the Chiefs sacked the opposing quarterback 57 times in the regular season, the second most in the league.

Spagnuolo leaned into his reputation, creating havoc for the quarterback while not surrendering long completions. The Chiefs blitzed on third down at the fifth-highest rate in the league (39.3 percent), plays that produced the third-highest pressure rate (64.3 percent), according to Next Gen Stats.

When a defensive back was part of Kansas City's blitzes, the unit produced nine sacks, the third most in the league, according to TruMedia. On such snaps, the Chiefs grabbed two interceptions and allowed just two touchdown passes, and the longest completion they surrendered was just 26 yards. Even while employing simulated pressures, the Chiefs had the most sacks from players in the secondary (nine).

"They get to the quarterback without having great personnel to do so, with Chris Jones being the exception," said Aaron Schatz, the chief analytics officer of

**RIGHT:** Defensive coordinator Steve Spagnuolo talks to cornerback Trent McDuffie during the Chiefs' January 7 win over the Los Angeles Rams. McDuffie excelled as the Chiefs' nickel defender.

FTN Network and inventor of DVOA. "They led the league in adjusted sack rate, which is sacks per pass play. The Ravens have more sacks (60), but the Chiefs faced fewer pass plays, which I think is a testament to Spagnuolo's scheme."

At age 64, Spagnuolo's goal each week is simple: Create as many blitzes as possible. The hope, Justin Reid said, is that the quarterback or opposing play caller won't know which type of blitz is coming at a pivotal moment.

"Nobody cares about if plays are made for them or not," Reid said. "It's about playing winning defense. It's about creating the opening for the next man to get the sack, getting on your man long enough that the next guy can make the play."

Spagnuolo's players understand that many of his blitzes are designed to collapse the pocket, requiring the defensive ends — Karlaftis, Danna and Charles Omenihu — and Jones, from the interior, to rush from the correct angle and with proper eye discipline so the quarterback cannot escape the trap.

The results? The Chiefs led the league with 73 unblocked pressures.

"Sometimes, there are some things that we do — and I know it when I call it — that can be a little risky," Spagnuolo said with a smile last month. "But it's a risk-reward, right?"

Spagnuolo's best blend of producing an effective pass rush, exceptional coverage and timely blitzes occurs when he employs dime personnel — six defensive backs, one linebacker and four linemen, a personnel grouping he used most in the league (185 snaps), according to TruMedia.

"We get to dime, you don't know what you're going to get from Coach Spags," defensive line coach Joe Cullen said in "Time's Yours 2," an NFL Films documentary released in September. "He does a great job of mixing it up. We could be bringing overload pressure, a strong safety coming or maybe the corner coming."

The Chiefs' dime personnel generated a league-leading 27 sacks and 92 "splash" plays (such as a turnover, sack, negative-yardage play or a pass breakup.)

"I really would not want to play our defense," quarterback Patrick Mahomes said. "We have great players all around, every single level. You have depth, guys that can rotate in and can do it all. And then you have Spags and his scheme. All the guys are so well-coached in the scheme that they use it to their advantage.

"It's hard to (get) a bead on what they're doing. That's why I knew in training camp. I was like, 'Man, I'm glad I don't have to play *those guys.*'"

———

Spagnuolo remembers his main objective when he joined the Chiefs: Just give head coach Andy Reid, Mahomes and the rest of the Chiefs' potent offense competency on defense.

In 2019, Spagnuolo was tasked with improving a unit that ranked 31st in total defense and surrendered 26.3 points per game. He installed his 4-3 under base system, a major change from the 3-4 defense used under former defensive coordinator Bob Sutton, and began overhauling the unit with general manager Brett Veach.

Spagnuolo and Veach acquired proven veterans, such as safety Tyrann Mathieu, linebacker Damien Wilson, cornerback Bashaud Breeland and defensive ends Frank Clark, Alex Okafor and Terrell Suggs. All were instrumental in Spagnuolo elevating the Chiefs to 12th in defensive DVOA.

Kansas City ended that season as Super Bowl LIV champions, hoisting the franchise's first Vince Lombardi Trophy in 50 years. Spagnuolo became the first defensive coordinator in NFL history to win the Super Bowl with two franchises after winning his first with the New York Giants.

But time moves quickly in the NFL, and in March 2022 the Chiefs began rebuilding their defense again, this time starting with a blockbuster trade. Receiver Tyreek Hill, the league's fastest player and the perfect game-changing deep threat for Mahomes, was sent to the Miami Dolphins for five draft picks.

The deal was a calculated gamble to balance the team's roster. With two first-round picks in the 2022 draft, the Chiefs selected cornerback Trent McDuffie (a first-team All-Pro this season) and Karlaftis. The next four defenders the Chiefs selected in the draft — safety Bryan Cook, linebacker Leo Chenal and cornerbacks Joshua Williams and Jaylen Watson — became either reliable starters or rotational contributors.

This past offseason, Veach continued to invest in the defense. Three of the Chiefs' four biggest acquisitions in free agency were Omenihu, Tranquill and safety Mike Edwards. The team created $9.6 million in salary-cap space by converting $12 million of Mahomes' $34.4 million roster bonus into a signing bonus. The Chiefs then used most of that to acquire Tranquill and Edwards and re-sign defensive tackle Derrick Nnadi.

In their first season with the Chiefs, the trio of Omenihu, Tranquill and Edwards have all played multiple positions, versatility that has given Spagnuolo the largest group of interchangeable players of his career. Omenihu collected a career-high seven sacks, Tranquill started eight games when Nick Bolton was injured and Edwards helped generate the Chiefs' two defensive touchdowns.

"With those three guys, the credit goes to Brett Veach and his (personnel staff)," Spagnuolo said. "That's one at each level. If you could bank on doing that every year in free agency, wouldn't that make a huge difference, right? What they've done stepping in speaks volumes to how important they've been."

Featuring eight starters drafted since 2020, the Chiefs finished the regular season ranked fifth in defensive EPA per play and seventh in defensive DVOA, the best marks during Spagnuolo's tenure. When this season started, the average age of the Chiefs' 12 projected defensive starters, (including nickel cornerback) was 24.8, the youngest in the league, according to Schatz.

"It's pretty surreal, the talent of the young guys around us now," said defensive tackle Mike Pennel, a 10-year veteran who was a member of the 2019 team. "This is the greatest defense that I've been a part of."

The defensive rookie who has played the most is Chamarri Conner, a safety the Chiefs moved up 15 spots to draft in the fourth round. In college, Conner played almost every position in Virginia Tech's secondary. Dave Merritt, the Chiefs' secondary coach, said Conner is the first rookie he's had in his 27 years in the NFL who has played four positions — free safety, strong safety, nickel and the third safety in the dime package.

"In OTAs, I was like, 'Man, this guy stinks; he can't go into (the) slot, there's no way,'" Merritt said of Conner. "Then, all of a sudden, he started climbing. He's growing where we would like him to grow."

Against the Bills, Conner played 76 of the Chiefs' 77 defensive snaps while replacing Edwards, who sustained a concussion on the game's second play. Conner finished with 10 tackles and a forced fumble. In coverage, he allowed just 25 yards as the nearest defender, earning him a 90.2 overall grade from Pro Football Focus, the highest of any safety who played in the divisional round.

As Spagnuolo walked off the field at Highmark Stadium, he wrapped his left arm around Conner, who smiled.

---

Spagnuolo's group doesn't have a nickname. The Chiefs defenders are not flashy. The secondary doesn't have a ballhawk.

**RIGHT:** Quarterbacks Blaine Gabbert and Patrick Mahomes share in a postgame celebration with defensive coordinator Steve Spagnuolo and defensive tackle Chris Jones.

Several defenders have acknowledged that they don't freelance as much as some of their peers who are looking to create a critical takeaway. Kansas City had just 17 takeaways in the regular season, tied for the fifth-fewest in the league. But Chiefs defenders are just as happy getting a third- or fourth-down stop as they are generating turnovers because of one reason: They have Mahomes, the league's best quarterback.

"The ability to get stops and prevent first downs is more predictive than the ability to get takeaways," Schatz said. "Takeaways are hugely important, but they're not as predictive. If what you want is consistent defense, being able to get stops is more important."

Earlier this month, when the defense had its first meeting ahead of the team's wild-card round game against the Dolphins, Spagnuolo informed his players that he would add more wrinkles to the game plan — new plays, blitzes and pre-snap checks — because he appreciated their collective intelligence.

"(Bolton) doesn't want vanilla, same with (Tranquill) and (Reid)," Spagnuolo said. "They want to be challenged mentally and they want to challenge the opponent's offense. Not all guys are like that. These guys are great that way."

During training camp last summer, L'Jarius Sneed told Spagnuolo he wanted to be the Chiefs' shadow cornerback — the defender who covers the opponent's best receiver — because he knew McDuffie could excel as the nickel defender. Sneed was correct. As the nearest defender in coverage on 90 targets in the regular season, Sneed didn't surrender a touchdown.

Operating from the slot, McDuffie led the Chiefs with five forced fumbles, in addition to recording seven pass breakups, three sacks and nine quarterback hits. He led all defensive backs with 14 unblocked pressures.

"Spags trusts us and I love that," McDuffie said. "I keep telling the coaches all the time, 'If you need me at safety, I can always do it.' I love when Spags gets to mess with the (opposing) offense. It's such a mind game with this defense. I've had a lot of fun."

The Chiefs' most memorable defensive highlight of the regular season came in a win over the Dolphins — and was ignited by McDuffie. When Miami quarterback Tua Tagovailoa threw a short pass to Hill behind the line of scrimmage, McDuffie recognized the play's design from film study and popped Hill a split-second after he caught the ball. Instead of recording a tackle for loss, McDuffie ripped the ball out of Hill's hands.

The ball rolled away from Hill and to Edwards, who knew he had no chance to sprint away from Hill. Edwards lateraled the ball to Cook, then protected his teammate by blocking tight end Durham Smythe. Cook went untouched 59 yards for a touchdown.

In the wild-card rematch against the Dolphins, the Chiefs' secondary played seven coverages, according to McDuffie, including one with him starting in his usual nickel spot before backpedaling to be one of the deep safeties.

The game featured one of Spagnuolo's best-disguised coverages. Edwards and Conner showed two-high coverage before rotating to a single-high look, with Conner as the deepest defender, before the snap. But after the snap, Edwards and Conner continued to rotate, switching back to two-high coverage. The play ended with Edwards intercepting Tagovailoa's intermediate pass.

In the second half, Dolphins coach Mike McDaniel voiced his frustration while watching the Chiefs defense limit his offense, which averaged 29.2 points on the season, to just seven.

"We can't do s—, man," McDaniel said.

Last week, Spagnuolo altered his tactics and his players responded. Almost every major contributor produced a winning play.

Jones was most disruptive as a defensive end, creating enough pressure to affect Allen's final two pass attempts, both of which fell incomplete. Karlaftis stopped one of the Bills' drives with a batted pass on third down. Allen's deepest pass of the game, with the ball traveling 52 yards past the line of scrimmage, fell incomplete because Reid was in the proper spot covering receiver Stefon Diggs.

Conner had his best performance of the season, five players recorded a tackle behind the line of scrimmage and the Bills never had a play of 20 or more yards.

Of course, Spagnuolo knew late Sunday night that the Chiefs were going from celebrating defeating one headache of an opposing quarterback in Allen to quickly preparing to face another in Lamar Jackson, the Baltimore Ravens' leader and this year's presumptive NFL MVP. Hoping to counterattack Jackson's rare skills, Spagnuolo's players expect his game plan — and his potential adjustments — will be his most complex of the season.

"Every week, there's something new," McDuffie said. ■

---

**LEFT:** Rookie safety Chamarri Conner takes instruction from Steve Spagnuolo following the Chiefs' final regular season game in Los Angeles.

# Championship Resolve

**Patrick Mahomes Remains Inevitable**

———————— BY ZAK KEEFER

While they stood and sang, he sat in silence. While the music thumped and the cigar smoke filled the air and his teammates danced amid the delirium of a fourth trip to the Super Bowl in five years, Patrick Mahomes retreated to a plastic chair in the corner of the visitor's locker room at M&T Bank Stadium and exhaled.

The elation was there, sure, but at this moment, the best football player on the planet wore a look of utter relief. For five minutes, he stared at his phone with a grin on his face.

Even after the midseason slog and all those drops by his receivers, after he spent weeks biting his tongue in front of the microphones only to finally erupt on the sideline, after his Pro Bowl tight end started showing his age and the pundits started to wonder if the champs still had the mettle to make another playoff run — this one would have to come on the road — one truth remains inevitable: this is still Patrick Mahomes' league.

He's Michael Jordan in his prime, the roadblock so many of his peers can't find their way around when it matters most. Jordan spent the 1990s crushing the title hopes of his counterparts — Patrick Ewing, Charles Barkley, Karl Malone — worthy Hall of Famers in their own right. That's what Mahomes is doing right now, leaving the likes of Josh Allen and Lamar Jackson asking themselves when their time is going to come. And if this guy's ever going to get out of the way.

"It's hard to describe someone that good," Kansas City general manager Brett Veach said Sunday night, an hour after the Chiefs gutted out a 17-10 win over the Ravens in the AFC Championship Game, their fourth conference title in Mahomes' six seasons as a starter. "He's a legend. He's a blessing."

And he remains an impediment for every team in the AFC with Super Bowl ambitions.

This run's been different — perhaps more gratifying — because of the road the Chiefs took. Because of a messy regular season and an offense that never looked right and the questions that lingered into early January. It was a little over a month ago that Veach huddled with head coach Andy Reid after the Chiefs dropped a game on Christmas Day to the Raiders, their fifth loss in eight weeks, an unimaginable skid of mediocrity for a team that's been a championship contender since the minute Mahomes became the starter in 2018.

"Something was off," Veach said. "That loss, I think it really hit us. It allowed the whole organization to take a look in the mirror."

Five weeks later, he called it one of the reasons they're still playing.

From the minute the postseason began, on a frigid evening in Kansas City in the wild-card round, the champs have looked revived. Kelce, for starters, seemed intent on shaking off his sloppy regular season: he stormed the field that night for warmups dancing and shouting, sleeveless in sub-zero temperatures. His energy never waned, and his fire lit the team. The Dolphins never had a chance.

What the Chiefs have done in consecutive weeks since, winning in Buffalo, then in Baltimore Sunday night, has been a testament to their championship resolve forged over postseason runs of the past, not to mention the lessons learned from their rocky regular season.

"It's a tough thing," Reid said of making deep playoff runs each winter, the grind of playing two or three extra games every year. "You got to work through that mentally. That's not easy."

Sunday's victory spoke to that. The Chiefs looked and played like the veteran team. The Ravens constantly got in their own way. The Chiefs committed three penalties; the Ravens eight. The Chiefs scored touchdowns on their first two red zone trips and finished without a turnover; the Ravens turned it over three times, twice deep in Kansas City territory.

Baltimore's frustration bubbled up throughout the game. Jackson threw an errant interception into triple coverage and slammed his helmet. Standout rookie Ravens receiver Zay Flowers fumbled the ball on the goal line, stormed to the bench and cut his hand.

The Chiefs played like champs.

"When it came time to put the hammer down, they put the hammer down," Reid said.

Mahomes sizzled early on, playing the quarterback position about as well as it can be played against an

**RIGHT:** Patrick Mahomes completed 30 of 39 passes against Baltimore, leading the Chiefs to their fourth conference title in Mahomes' six seasons as a starter.

elite defense like Baltimore's. He made tight-window throws, like his first-quarter touchdown to Kelce. He scrambled from muddy pockets and kept drives alive. He completed his first 11 passes, a harsh and humbling reminder for a raucous purple-and-black-clad crowd at M&T Bank Stadium.

That is, the AFC still runs through the Chiefs — even if the games are played somewhere besides Kansas City.

"We're the outlaws," wideout Rashee Rice boasted later. "Everybody wants to beat the Chiefs. We got a target on our backs every day."

After a grind of a second half that saw five straight punts from the Chiefs offense, Mahomes lofted his prettiest throw of the game, an arching dagger to Marquez Valdes-Scantling on 3rd and 9 with 2:19 left that sent those fans filing to the exits.

"We got the best quarterback in the world," Chiefs linebacker Drue Tranquill said. "We got the best tight end in the world. We got the best coach in the world. We got the best defensive coordinator in the world. We got the best general manager in the world.

"When you have all of that? It's only a matter of time."

At one point in the second half, Mahomes had 27 completions to Jackson's five. Mahomes finished 30-for-39 for 241 yards and a touchdown, outplaying the league's presumptive MVP in moments big and small (Jackson was 20-for-37 for a touchdown and an interception). In a game where both quarterbacks faced off against championship-level defenses, Mahomes was steadier. Jackson was streaky at best.

And a crowd that desperately wanted to see Jackson finally advance to a Super Bowl — just about all that's missing from his resume at this point — instead had to watch No. 15 punch a fourth trip in five years, with a chance to win his third Lombardi Trophy. With Joe Burrow's 2021 season being the lone exception, Mahomes continues to send his counterparts home, year after year.

The scene afterward was something, familiar in some respects but fresh in others. Mahomes stood on another stage, accepting another trophy, perhaps the most surprising of all the ones he's hoisted during this gilded start to his career. "You don't take it for granted," he said later of advancing to his latest Super Bowl. "You never know how many you're going to get to."

He's 28. He's already won 14 playoff games, same as Peyton Manning, same as John Elway, same as Terry

---

**RIGHT:** Chris Jones takes down Ravens quarterback Lamar Jackson in the first half. The Chiefs sacked Jackson four times, limiting Baltimore to just a field goal over the game's final three quarters.

*"He gives everyone that belief and that hope. It doesn't matter what the odds are, where we're playing, where we're going. If we have 15 under center, we have a shot."*

Bradshaw. That puts him tied for third all-time, behind only Joe Montana (16 wins) and Tom Brady (35). And he's done this in just six seasons.

After Mahomes handed the Lamar Hunt trophy off, Kelce — who caught all 11 of his targets for 116 yards and a touchdown — strolled from the stage hand-in-hand with celebrity girlfriend Taylor Swift. One Chiefs teammate couldn't wrap his mind around the crush of photographers, dozens and dozens deep, following them. It was staggering, even for a team accustomed to dealing with an intense spotlight.

"My God, I've never seen anything like this," the player said.

From there, Kelce finally found his brother, Jason, who wore a Chiefs beanie. They hugged.

"This is an easy team to root for," Jason said a moment later. "They stayed together through all the nonsense."

There was plenty of it, the rigors of a championship chase that for months never seemed on track. The sparks came, from Kelce, who was edgy in walkthroughs and practices all week ("He led us," Mahomes said, "he loves the challenge"). And from Reid, who never flinched in his postgame meetings with team owner Clark Hunt this season ("He never doubted the team," said Hunt). And from defensive coordinator Steve Spagnuolo, who scripted a masterpiece of a game plan Sunday, stifling Jackson and the Ravens' offense all game long.

But — same with every contender — so much of it rests on the face of the franchise, who after the most exasperating season of his career, found a seat in a celebratory locker room to sit alone and soak it in.

It wasn't just another trip to the Super Bowl. It was the most improbable one of all.

"He gives everyone that belief and that hope," Veach said of his quarterback. "It doesn't matter what the odds are, where we're playing, where we're going. If we have 15 under center, we have a shot." ■

**RIGHT:** Patrick Mahomes hoists the Lamar Hunt Trophy for the fourth time in his career following the Chiefs' win over Baltimore to advance to Super Bowl LVIII.

# The Athletic

Steven Ginsberg, Executive Editor

Sarah Goldstein, Editorial Director - NFL

Alison Cotsonika, Senior Managing Editor - NFL

Dan Uthman, Senior Managing Editor - Talent Development

Adam Hirshfield, Deputy Managing Editor - NFL

Mike Sansone, Senior Editor - NFL

Jimmy Durkin, Senior Editor - NFL

Stephen Cohen, Enterprise Editor - NFL

Amy Cavenaile, Editorial Director - Design and Visuals

Trevor Gibbons, Head of Commercial Strategy

Rosalie Pisano, Commercial Partnerships

Eric Drobny, Creative Development Director

Brooks Varni, Creative Development

Jerry Fagerberg, Product Manager

Ryan Cole, Social Manager

Tyler Sutton, Senior Marketing Manager

Keenan Williams, Marketing Manager

Gwenna Wagoner, Design

Jade Hurrle, Design

**FEATURED WRITERS FROM THE ATHLETIC**

Nate Taylor, Dan Pompei, Zak Keefer
Special thanks to the entire The Athletic NFL Staff